Companion to the Qur'ān

William Montgomery Watt

ONEWORLD
OXFORD

By the same author

The Faith and Practice of Al-Ghazálí
Islamic Fundamentalism and Modernity
The Influence of Islam upon Mediaeval Europe
Islamic Political Thought
Islamic Philosophy and Theology
Muhammad at Medina
Muhammad: Prophet and Statesman
What is Islam?

COMPANION TO THE QUR'ĀN

Oneworld Publications
(Sales and Editorial)
185 Banbury Road
Oxford OX2 7AR
England

Oneworld Publications
(U.S. Sales Office)
42 Broadway
Rockport, MA 01966
USA

A CIP record for this book is available
from the British Library

ISBN 1–85168–036–5

Printed and bound by
WSOY, Finland

FOREWORD

This reissue of the *Companion to the Qur'ān* could not come at a more appropriate time. It is now widely and increasingly recognized that it is of the utmost importance for the future of the human race that the world's great religions draw closer to one another, and that each, while retaining its own distinctive position, should strive for a fuller positive appreciation of the others. Such an understanding is to be particularly desired for Islam and Christianity.

I have always taken the view that Muḥammad genuinely believed that the messages he received (and which constitute the Qur'ān) came to him from God. I hesitated for a time to speak of Muḥammad as a prophet, because this would have been misunderstood by Muslims who took the traditional Islamic view of prophethood, according to which the Qur'ān, as the speech of God Himself, is infallible. Now, however, I think it important to state publicly that I believe Muḥammad to have been a prophet on a similar level to the Old Testament prophets. When earlier Christian scholars looked at the Qur'ān they found many Old Testament stories, and because of this and their belief that Islam was a false religion, they took the view that the Qur'ān was a mere hotch-potch of biblical material pieced together by Muḥammad himself.

A more mature scholarship shows that this view is ridiculous. If we look carefully at the Qur'ān, what strikes us is not how much knowledge it shows of the Bible, but how little. A few of the more colourful stories in Genesis and Exodus appear several times, often with non-biblical additions and alterations; but that is about all. There is much about Moses, but there is no clear appreciation of the exodus and of its importance in Jewish religion, or even of the fact that the great work of Moses was to secure the deliverance of the Hebrew people from a state of serfdom in Egypt and to lead them to the borders of the land promised by God. There is nothing about the settlement in Palestine. David is mentioned, but there is no realization that he was above all a war leader who created a powerful kingdom. Solomon is spoken of, but not as a great king renowned for his wisdom. There is nothing about the two kingdoms, or the exile and return from exile, and nothing about the great prophets and their achievements. When it comes to the New Testament, the Qur'ān has a version of the Lucan account of the Virgin Birth, but apart from that shows no knowledge of Christian teaching and of the formation of the Church.

When it is realized how little was known by Muḥammad and the Meccan Arabs of the Jewish and Christian religions, the remarkable achievement of the Qur'ān can be recognized. It may be said that it presents in its own way all the main truths of the religion of Abraham, which is followed also by Jews and Christians. I maintain that the only reasonable explanation of this fact is that Muḥammad was as truly inspired by God as were the Old Testament prophets. Moreover, while the latter were for the most part critics of an existing religion as it was being practised, Muḥammad had the mission of bringing belief in God to people with virtually no religion.

Some Muslims today try to distinguish their religion from Judaism and Christianity by saying they worship not God but Allāh. It may be allowed that the Muslim conception of God differs in some ways from that of Jews and Christians; but the object of worship is not a conception but a being, and Allāh is merely the Arabic word for this being, called God in English and Deus in Latin; and there are Arabic-speaking Jews and Christians who also worship Allāh.

Christians cannot, of course, accept the assertion in surā 4.156/7 that 'they [the Jews] did not slay him [Jesus]' if this is taken to mean that Jesus did not die on the cross; and such has been the standard interpretation among Muslims. This and the surrounding verses are directed against the Jews and not the Christians, and Christians would agree that the crucifixion was not a Jewish victory. Some Muslim scholars are now suggesting interpretations of the passage which do not deny that Jesus died.

For readers who are using a different translation of the Qur'ān it may be worth setting down some words of Arthur Arberry from the introduction to his translation.

> This task [of translating] was undertaken,
> not lightly, and carried to its conclusion at

> a time of great personal distress, through
> which it comforted and sustained the writer
> in a manner for which he will always be
> grateful. He therefore acknowledges his
> gratitude to whatever power or Power
> inspired the man and the Prophet who first
> recited these scriptures.

It may also be noted that the Roman Catholic Church in one of the documents of the Second Vatican Council fully accepted Muslims as fellow-worshippers of the God of Abraham, expressed a desire for greater mutual understanding and hoped that Muslims and Christians could work together to promote peace, justice and morality.

In this reissue there have been one or two slight additions to the commentary. The introduction is reproduced as it was, except that I have substituted for Richard Bell's *Introduction to the Qur'ān* my revision of that work under the title: Watt and Bell, *Introduction to the Qur'ān*, Edinburgh University Press, 1970.

W. Montgomery Watt
1994

CONTENTS

INTRODUCTION

About the year AD 610 a merchant in a moderate way at Mecca, called Muḥammad, began to have religious experiences. More particularly there were times when he found in his heart certain words, constituting shorter or longer passages of rhythmic prose with rhyme or assonance; and from various circumstances he became convinced that these passages were messages or revelations from God which he had to communicate to the people of Mecca. The revelations continued until Muḥammad's death in 632. His proclamation of the message led to a religious movement which was the origin of the religion of Islam, and also of a vast political state or body politic which for a century or so may be called the Arab Empire.[1]

The revelations were at first carried mainly in the memories of Muḥammad and his followers, and passages were repeated in the course of public worship. The Arabic word *qur'ān* is probably derived from, or at least regarded as an equivalent of, a Syriac word *qeryāna* meaning the lection or portion of Scripture to be read or recited in the course of worship. Since the Qur'ān itself speaks of 'a Book', it is probable that Muḥammad himself began to arrange the revelations to form a book. The complete collection of all the fragmentary revelations, however, was not accomplished until about 650 in the reign of the caliph 'Uthmān (644–56). This 'Uthmānic recension gave the Qur'ān the form in which we now have it in respect of its order, contents and main divisions. The older commentators mention a number of variant readings which were excluded by 'Uthmān's recension. Even among the great majority who accepted the 'Uthmānic text, variations arose in points of detail, such as vocalization, or the precise form of a word. Shortly after the year 900, as the result of the efforts of a scholar Ibn-Mujāhid, seven sets of readings were recognized as canonical, each in two slightly different versions (listed in Bell and Watt, *Introduction to the Qur'ān*, 49). Not all fourteen sets have been equally popular. At the present time one set of readings—

[1] A brief account of Muḥammad's career will be found in Montgomery Watt, *Muḥammad Prophet and Statesman.*

those of the Kufan scholar 'Āṣim in the version of Ḥafṣ—have been widely accepted as the standard readings and are adopted in the Egyptian official editions. The differences of reading, even the non-canonical ones, are all of minor importance, and do not affect the general teaching of the Qur'ān; an example of a case where there is a slight difference will be found in the comment on 81.24.

The Qur'ān is arranged in suras or chapters, each of which is divided into verses. The division into suras (Ar. *sūra*) probably goes back to Muḥammad himself. Each sura has a name, derived from a distinctive phrase in the sura; e.g. sura 2, 'The sura of the Cow', gets it name from the reference to a cow in verse 67/3 and the following verses. Some suras have many different names, but most are seldom used, and only one or two common variants have been mentioned here. There have also been variations in the division of the suras into verses, and consequently in the numbering of the verses. This *Companion* gives both the numbering of the Egyptian official edition and—after a stroke where it is different—that of the European edition of Gustav Flügel, which is adopted by most European books up till about 1950. (It should be noted that the numbers are never more than seven apart; thus 39/33 is shortened to 39/3, 110/12 to 110/2, and so on; but numbers below 20 are not abbreviated, so that 11/18 is always written so, and not as 11/8.)

The aim of the present *Companion* is to provide the English reader with the chief background material needed to facilitate the understanding and appreciation of the Qur'ān in translation. Such material falls under two heads, namely, that concerning questions of translation, and that concerning questions of interpretation.

(1) The Arabic language is such that there are often several different ways of 'taking' a sentence, and these ways yield at least slightly different meanings. An English example would be the phrase in a well-known prayer 'God, whose property is always to have mercy ...'. The question may be asked whether the adverb 'always' is to be taken with 'is' or with 'to have mercy'; that is to say, whether the words mean that 'God always has the property of having mercy', or that 'God

has the property of always having mercy'. It might further be said that the first alternative gave 'always' the sense of 'eternally', and the second the sense of 'temporally on appropriate occasions'. This kind of thing occurs much more frequently in Qur'ānic Arabic, and there is often something to be said for each of several possibilities. Normally, however, the translator can only express one in English; and thus something of the suggestiveness of the Qur'ān is inevitably lost. The present *Companion* mentions a few of the alternatives in order to illustrate this richness of the Qur'ānic language. A similar difficulty occurs where an Arabic word has connotations which cannot be brought out by a single English word. One of the hardest to render is the Arabic word *muslim*. It hovers between the later technical sense of 'Muslim', and the non-technical sense of 'one surrendering or submitting'. The translator is probably correct in choosing a non-technical rendering, but the reader of the translation ought to be aware that in many cases something near the technical sense is also suggested by the Arabic. Yet other cases occur where no English word can convey the full meaning of the Arabic. Thus the word *kasaba* is translated 'he earned', because in the Qur'ān the word usually means 'he performed an act by which he earned merit or demerit on the Day of Judgement'. Until the reader is aware of this the translation will puzzle and mislead him. Yet to translate 'he acted' or 'he did' would omit something of the meaning of the Arabic. A. J. Arberry has been careful to preserve a high degree of consistency in his translation, and, where a word is puzzling, the reader will sometimes be helped by the Index to the Commentary, which may give a reference to another passage where the word is explained.

(2) Once the precise meaning of the text has been determined, or the alternatives indicated, there arises the question of interpretation. To what particular persons or incidents does a verse refer? Who are 'those in whose hearts is sickness'? Is the assertion that 'God has no offspring' directed against pagans who believe in 'daughters of God' or Christians who speak of 'the son of God'? Muslim scholars collected much material about 'the occasions of revelation', that is, the inci-

dents or circumstances with reference to which the revelations came to Muḥammad. Many of these are certainly correct; others are dubious, being probably only the conjectures of scholars who lived a century or two after Muḥammad. The most assured of these 'occasions' have been mentioned. These are supplemented by careful study of the text in connection with the material given in the biographies of Muḥammad.

The Arberry translation uses a simple form of transliteration of Arabic names, in accordance with the popular audience to whom it is directed. For a Commentary, however, a more scholarly system of transliteration seems appropriate and that has therefore been adopted.

The following shortened forms have been used for books referred to several times:

Bell, *Origin*: Richard Bell, *The Origin of Islam in its Christian Environment*, London, 1926.

EI[1]: *Encyclopaedia of Islam*, first edition.

EI[2]: *Encyclopaedia of Islam*, new edition.

Ibn-Hishām: *Sīrat Rasūl Allāh*, ed. F. Wüstenfeld, Göttingen, 1859–60.

Jeffery, *Materials*: Arthur Jeffery, *Materials for the History of the Text of the Qur'ān*, Leiden, 1937.

Kamal, *Sacred Journey*: Ahmad Kamal, *The Sacred Journey, being Pilgrimage to Makkah*, London, 1964 (English and Arabic; reference to the English paging).

Lane, *Lexicon*: E. W. Lane, *Arabic–English Lexicon*, London, 1863–93.

Nöldeke-Schwally: Th. Nöldeke, *Geschichte des Qorans*, second edition, ed. by F. Schwally, etc., Leipzig, 1909–38.

Watt, *Islam and Integration*: W. Montgomery Watt, *Islam and the Integration of Society*, London, 1961.

Mecca: id., *Muhammad at Mecca*, Oxford, 1953.

Medina: id., *Muhammad at Medina*, Oxford, 1956.

Prophet: id., *Muhammad, Prophet and Statesman*, London, 1961.

Watt and Bell, *Introduction*: id. and Richard Bell, *Introduction to the Qur'ān*, Edinburgh, 1970.

I

THE OPENING

Al-fātiḥa

This sura consists of a prayer or act of worship, and is used daily by Muslims in the Ṣalāt or formal worship and on many other occasions. Its function is in some ways similar to that of the Lord's Prayer of Christians. Since it thus differs in character from the rest of the Qur'ān, some early Muslims thought it was an individual prayer of Muḥammad's, and it was omitted from the codices of Ibn-'Abbās and Ibn-Mas'ūd. It is appropriate that it should be placed at the beginning of the Qur'ān, and the name by which it is generally known reflects this position. It has also had several other names. It is regarded by Muslims as giving the quintessence of Islamic doctrine. Because of its special character it is difficult to date, but the probability is that it is fairly early, about the fourth year of Muḥammad's mission, or AD 613.

1 In the name of God: this invocation (the *Bismillah*) is placed before all the suras except one, but only here is it counted as a verse. It is also used by Muslims before all important actions. There is no great difference between the adjectives rendered 'merciful', 'compassionate' (*raḥmān, raḥīm*), though a distinction of emphasis is sometimes made.

2 Lord of all Being: literally 'of the worlds', but probably to be taken as 'of all the spheres of being'. It is sometimes said to refer particularly to men, jinn and angels.

6 the straight path: Ar. *aṣ-ṣirāṭ al-mustaqīm*; usually taken to be the religion of Islam.

7 *those against whom thou art wrathful . . . those who are astray:* Jews and Christians respectively according to a traditional interpretation, but this is not possible if the sura is early Meccan, while the phrases would suit the pagan Arabs. Similar phrases in 5.60/5 ('with whom he is wroth'), 5.77/81 ('who went astray'), etc. may be a new application to Medinan opponents of terms first applied to Meccan polytheists.

❦ 2 ❦

THE COW

Al-baqara

This is the longest sura. Most of the passages composing it belong to the first two or three years after the Hijra. The name comes from the incident in verses 67/63 to 71/66.

1 – 7/6 Believers and unbelievers

1 Alif Lam Mim: the names of Arabic letters. No satisfactory explanation has been given of the occurrence of these letters at the beginning of many suras. For the various theories, cf. Watt and Bell, *Introduction*, 61–5.

2/1 the Book: the written scripture, giving the Arabs in essentials what was already in the hands of Jews and Christians, who were called 'the people of the Book'.

3/2 the Unseen: literally, 'the absent', but often referring to supernatural matters, such as God, judgement, Paradise. The word could also be taken adverbially, namely, 'who believe (in what is revealed) although they do not see it'.

expend: probably implying it is to support needy Muslims.

that we have provided them: what we have given them as food, drink and covering; God's 'provision' or 'sustenance' (*rizq*) was an important conception among the Arabs.

4/3 What has been sent down before thee: previous revelations to Jews, Christians and others. These were believed by the Muslims to be identical in essence with the Qur'ān.

5/4 prosper: are successful in the deepest sense; understood by Muslims as entering Paradise.

6/5 those who have disbelieved: probably refers to Jews, since there were few atheists at Medina.

7/6 has set a seal on their hearts: expresses the inscrutability of their failure to respond to Muḥammad's message.

8/7 – 20/19 Pretended believers

8/7 who say 'we believe . . .' but they are not believers: probably refers to those Arabs of Medina, later called 'hypocrites', who outwardly acknowledged Muḥammad as prophet, but disapproved of his growing political power. Some Jews also might be included here.

9/8 and they are not aware: that is, they deceive themselves without realizing it.

10/9 in their hearts there is a sickness: a phrase which for a time was a standard description of those who subsequently became 'hypocrites'.

11/10 do not corruption: probably means, do not criticize the revelations and lower the morale of the community.

13/12 as the people believe: the community of Muslims in Medina.

14/13 Satans: devils or demons; probably metaphorical for their leaders, or the leaders of the opposition to Muḥammad.

16/15 error . . . guidance: they have bartered the true guidance proclaimed by Muḥammad for their present erroneous views.

21/19 – 29/7 Appeals and arguments addressed to unbelievers

21/19 O you men: this form of address is generally held to be Meccan, since in Medina the common form was 'O you believers'.

22/0 edifice: a building covering you over, like a dome.

compeers: do not recognize deities beside the supreme deity, God.

23/1 a sura like it: this challenge implies that a proof of the divine origin of the Qur'ān is its inimitability, later called its *i'jāz* or miraculous character.

24/2 stones: some commentators suggest idols, but perhaps the idea is that the heat of Hell will be increased by brimstone.

25/3 gardens: Paradise or Heaven.

underneath: that is, through; Arabic speaks in this way since the water in a stream is always lower than the banks.

were provided before: were given as sustenance on earth; the following words are not clear but may mean that the fruits of paradise are similar to the earthly but are perfect of their kind.

26/4 God is not ashamed: apparently due to the fact that Muḥammad's opponents had ridiculed the mention of the spider (29.41/40), the fly (22.73/72) and other small insects.

27/5 The covenant of God: sometimes said to be the covenant with the Jews at Sinai, but this would be unlikely if the passage is Meccan.

28/6 seeing you were dead: in the state of non-existence before birth.

shall be returned: that is, for the Judgement.

30/28 – 39/7 Story of Adam, Iblis and the Fall

30/28 viceroy: Ar. *khalīfa,* 'deputy', *sc.* Adam.

that you know not: what you know not.

34/2 bow yourselves: Ar. *usjudū,* the word used for touching the ground with the forehead in ritual prayer: such corporeal gestures are still used as marks of respect in the east.

36/4 Satan: perhaps not a proper name, but simply 'the demon': in any case identical with Iblīs.

37/5 turned towards him: relenting.

40/38 – 48/5 Appeals to the Children of Israel

41/38 that I have sent down: that is, the Qur'ān.

confirming that which is with you: the Jewish Bible (Old Testament).

My signs: the word 'sign' (*āya*) can also mean 'verse of the Qur'ān': the meaning presumably is, 'Do not exchange belief in this new revelation for something valueless'.

42/39 do not conceal the truth: the Muslims believed that the Jews were concealing verses foretelling the prophethood of Muḥammad.

43/0 perform the prayer: the ritual prayer or Ṣalāt, which includes actions such as standing, bowing (or inclining one's head—*rukū'*) and prostrating oneself (*sujūd*). This, with the paying of the legal alms (*zakāt*), a kind of tithe, were the external marks of a community which had become Muslim.

44/1 bid others to piety . . . forget: the Jews of Medina who had previously called on pagans to believe in God, now argue against God's revelation to Muḥammad.

the Book: the Old Testament or Torah.

47/4 *have preferred you above all beings:* by sending revelations to them; the uniqueness of Israel's vocation is in some sense recognized.

48/5 *neither shall they be helped:* Muslim apologists say this means that the fact of being a Jew will not help a man in Judgement.

49/6 – 62/59 The deliverance from Pharaoh and the perversity of the Israelites

49/6 *And when . . .:* this is the literal rendering of a frequent Qur'ānic usage which can hardly be adequately represented in English. Sometimes a word like 'remember' is said to be understood. The word *idh,* 'when', seems to be a form from the noun meaning 'time'. We might say 'once' or 'there was a time when', or perhaps omit any English equivalent.

your sons: cf. the order to kill the male children in *Exodus,* ch. 1.

51/48 *the Calf:* as a god; cf. *Exodus,* ch. 32.

53/0 *the Book:* the essential revelation as it was given to all prophets.

the Salvation: Ar. *furqān.* Modern scholars regard this word as derived from the Syriac *purqānā,* 'salvation', but influenced in meaning by the Arabic *faraqa* 'separate, distinguish'. It occurs at six other places in the Qur'ān: 2.185/1; 3.3/2; 8.29, 41/2; 2.48/9; 25.1. In most of these it is referred to as given or sent down by God along with a Book (to Moses or Muḥammad); but 8.41/2 speaks of 'the day of the *furqān,* the day the two hosts encountered'. This must be the battle of Badr. It would therefore appear that the meaning is something like 'salvation' or 'deliverance' *sc.* from Judgement, and this distinguishes or marks off believers from unbelievers. Cf. Bell, *Origin*, 118–25; R. Paret, art. 'Furḳān' in *EI*².

54/1 turn to your Creator: sc. in repentance.

slay one another: literally 'slay yourselves' but the commentators agree that it must mean one another and some hold it means that the just are to slay the wicked. Cf. *Exodus*, 32.27, 'slay every man his brother, and every man his companion, and every man his neighbour'.

55/2 see God openly: cf. *Exodus*, 19.21, 'gaze'.

56/3 We raised you up: Muslim commentators tell a story of how the seventy men chosen to help Moses heard God speak to him, but were not satisfied and wanted to see God. They were struck by lightning, but on Moses' intercession were restored to life by God. This appears to be from Talmudic Jewish sources.

57/4 manna and quails: cf. *Exodus*, 16; *Numbers*, 11.

58/5 Unburdening: they were to say the word 'Unburdening' (*ḥiṭṭa*) as a prayer for forgiveness, but some ridiculed the act, perhaps by substituting a similar-sounding but blasphemous word.

60/57 twelve fountains: the commentators say there was one for each of the tribes, and that this is the 'drinking-place' referred to; cf. *Exodus*, 17; *Numbers*, 20, where there is no mention of 'twelve'.

61/58 green herbs . . .: cf. *Numbers*, 11.4,5. For 'corn' (*fūm*) there was a variant reading *thūm*, 'garlic', found in Ibn-Mas'ūd, etc. (cf. Jeffery, *Materials*, 26), and approved by the commentator az-Zamakhsharī (ad loc.) as more appropriate; garlic is mentioned in *Numbers*, 11.5.

62/59 Sabaeans: Ar. *Ṣābi'īn*. The original reference may have been to the Mandaeans of southern Iraq, but this is not certain. Later the name was applied to a sect with its centre at Ḥarrān in northern Iraq, which produced distinguished scholars in the Greek tradition of philosophy, astronomy and mathematics, but was polytheistic, worshipping moon and stars. This sect may have falsely claimed to be the Sabaeans of the Qur'ān in order to avoid persecution.

their wage awaits them: that is, they will go to heaven. This verse has been a centre of controversy. Some Muslim scholars interpreted it as applying only to those Jews, Christians and other believers in God and the Last Day who accepted Islam. Others said it had been abrogated by such a verse as 3.85/79, 'who so desires another religion than Islam . . . in the next world he shall be among the losers'. In so far as the other religions are identical in essentials with the religion Muḥammad preached, the Qur'ānic view would be that those who practised them would go to heaven.

63/0 – 74/69 The perversity of the Jews

63/0 with you: still addressed to the Children of Israel.

raised the Mount: the commentators refer to a story (based on Jewish tradition) that, when the Israelites would not accept the law given to Moses, God lifted up mount Sinai and held it over their heads to terrify them.

take forcefully: resolutely accept as binding on you.

65/1 transgressed the Sabbath: the commentators tell the following story to explain this verse and 7.163–66; in the days of David the fish at Elath (Ayla) on the Red Sea used to come to shore on the Sabbath to tempt Israelites living there, but kept away on other days; some Israelites broke the sabbath and caught them or made canals which could be closed so as to trap them; others kept the sabbath and tried to stop the sabbath-breakers, but in vain; at length David cursed the latter and they were turned into apes, then after three days swept into the sea by a wind. This story has not been traced in Jewish legend.

67/3 commands you to sacrifice a cow: this passage is obscure; the story told to explain it is that after a man had been murdered, Moses ordered the sacrifice of a cow of a particular kind; only the heifer of a certain orphan answered the description, and he was given a large price; when the dead man was struck with part of the animal, he revived for long enough to name his murderer. Modern scholars think the passage may be connected with *Numbers*, 19.1–9, and *Deuteronomy*, 21.1–9.

72/67 when you killed: the 'you' is plural.

75/0 – 82/76 Jewish craft and false pride

75/0 Are you then so eager: addressing the Muslims.

tampered with it: Ar. *yuḥarrifūna-hā*, later interpreted as 'corrupted it'. This is one of the verses on which is based the later Islamic doctrine that Jews and Christians have 'corrupted' their scriptures. The Qur'ān itself, however, does not assert any general corruption, but seems to speak only of playing with words in a blasphemous way, and also of concealing verses, such as those alleged by Muslims to be prophesies of the coming of Muḥammad. Cf. F. Buhl, art. *'taḥrīf'* in *EI*[1], and Watt, *Islam and Integration*, 259–66.

76/1 dispute with you before your Lord: this should mean in heaven, where the argument could be that the Jews knew Muḥammad was a prophet, yet did not follow him; but it would also be appropriate to take it as meaning that some Jews told others not to give the Muslims too much information about the scriptures lest they get the better of them in argument.

78/3 common folk: Ar. *ummiyyūn*, almost certainly representing the Jewish conception of 'gentiles'; this sense fits the present verse with the words 'not knowing the Book'; it also fits the references to Muḥammad as the *ummī* prophet, i.e. gentile or non-Jewish; e.g. 7.157/6. Later Muslim apologetic, to enhance the miraculous character of the Qur'ān, insisted that Muḥammad was illiterate, and supported this by interpreting *ummī* as 'illiterate'. While most scholars now agree that Muḥammad had not read any Jewish or Christian writings, the original meaning of *ummī* was rather 'gentile'. In the present verse the reference might be to Arabs attached to the Jews of Medina. Cf. Watt, *Medina*, 178.

fancies: the exact meaning is uncertain.

79/3 write the Book: a traditional interpretation is that they transcribe the Bible corruptly, but it is conceivable that there is rather a reference to Jewish tradition.

earnings: that is, punishment in Hell.

80/74 a number of days: the Jews are said to have held that no Jew would be in Hell for more than a limited period (some said forty days, others less than a year).

covenant: that is, has God promised you . . .?

81/75 earns: or 'does', but with the connotation that he thereby earns punishment in Hell. Later theologians held that the only evil which led to eternal punishment in Hell was idolatry or abandonment of Islam.

83/77 – 103/97 Jewish disobedience and unbelief

83/77 took compact: made the covenant of Sinai.

85/79 killing one another: the Jewish clans at Medina were on different sides in the fighting there before the Hijra, and so shared in killing their fellow-Jews and expelling them from habitations (or lands).

you ransom them: the Jews fulfil this command of the Book, but neglect the prohibition of killing Jews.

87/1 clear signs: Ar. *bayyināt*; could here be the miracles, but is usually 'evidences', verbal in character.

the Holy Spirit: Ar. *rūḥ al-qudus*; some commentators say this means Gabriel (cf. 97.4); in general the Qur'ān shows little awareness of Christian teaching about the Spirit.

and some slay: the primary reference may be to Jesus.

88/2 Our hearts are uncircumcised: the heart is the seat of knowledge and understanding; 'uncircumcised' is said to be used metaphorically for 'covered' and so not open to receive the message. Some commentators interpret 'covered' as 'filled' and so requiring nothing from Muḥammad's message.

89/3 confirming: the Qur'ān confirms previous revelations.

prayed for victory: before the Hijra the Jews are said to have prayed that God would help them against the unbelievers by the expected prophet (the Messiah).

93/87 raised over you ... forcefully: cf. verse 63/0.

We hear and rebel: instead of 'we hear and do (or obey)'; apparently they played on the resemblance between Arabic '*aṣaynā, we rebel,* and the Hebrew '*asīnū, we do.*

made to drink the Calf: cf. *Exodus,* 32.20, Moses 'ground it to powder and strawed it upon the water, and made the children of Israel drink of it'.

94/88 yours exclusively: suggesting the Jewish concept of the Chosen People.

not for other people: literally, 'not for the people', with a suggestion of gentiles (Hebrew, *ummōt*; Latin, *gentes*; Greek, *ethnē*).

long for death: the point is that, if the Jews are certain of heaven, then, since heaven is better, they should long for it;

but they do not do this because they fear punishment for the evil deeds which 'their hands have forwarded' and which will be included in the reckoning.

96/0 thou shalt find them: the passage is grammatically disjointed. Another possible interpretation is: 'Thou (Muḥammad) shalt find them (the Jews) the most eager of men for life, even (more eager) than the idolaters; one of them (the Jews) wishes . . .'

97/1 an enemy to Gabriel: the Jews are said to have asked Muḥammad which angel brought the revelation to him; when he said 'Gabriel', they replied that he was their enemy and a messenger of war and punishment; had it been Michael they would have believed because he was their friend and a messenger of peace and plenty.

brought it: sc. the Qur'ān.

98/2 Messengers: or 'apostles', that is, those who transmitted messages (revelations) from God to their fellows, and so roughly equal to 'prophet' in Judaeo-Christian usage. Muḥammad's title among Muslims is 'the Messenger of God' (*rasūl Allāh*), and it is only in European languages that he is commonly called 'prophet'.

ungodly: Ar. *fāsiqūn,* usually meaning those Muslims or other monotheists who sin by omission or commission.

102/96 Solomon: the devils, having failed to tempt Solomon to sin, tried to destroy his reputation; they wrote books of magic and hid them under his throne, then after his death said this was the source of his power over men and spirits. This slander was denied by the Qur'ān.

Hārūt and Mārūt: two angels sent down by the angelic council to be judges on earth; when Zuhra (or Venus) appeared before them as a beautiful woman, they were carried away by desire for her, and tried to follow her to heaven; on being given a choice between punishment in this life or the life to come, they chose the former and are kept suspended by the feet in Babylon, where those who want to learn magic can hear their voice.

without they said: without first saying.

what hurt them: the sorcery and magic they learned lead to eternal punishment.

104/98 – 110/04 The believers are warned against the Jews

104/98 Observe us . . . Regard us . . .: the point appears to be that the Muslims had been following the Jews in using the word *rā'inā* in prayers, in the meaning 'observe us' or 'listen to us', but that the Jews mispronounced the Arabic word (cf. Lane, *Lexicon, s.v. ra'ā,* 4) to confuse it with the Hebrew word *ra'*, 'bad', 'evil'. The believers are therefore told to use another word *unẓurnā,* which can only mean 'regard us'.

106/0 whatever verse we abrogate or cast into oblivion: Muḥammad's opponents at Medina are said to have criticized the fact that the commands of God apparently changed, and that is in a sense admitted. On the basis of this verse, however (and of others such as 16.101/3), Muslim jurists built up an elaborate theory of 'abrogation' (*naskh*), according to which certain commands in the Qur'ān had been cancelled or 'abrogated', and replaced by others. The reason might be that circumstances had changed. Thus the command at Mecca to spend a large part of the night in prayer was relaxed in Medina where Muḥammad and his followers had responsible work to do by day; the verses with the command (73.1–4) are 'abrogated' by another (73.20). Cf. Bell, *Introduction,* 98 f. The words 'cast into oblivion' suggest that some verses from what was revealed have not been retained in the present Qur'ān, but from the nature of the case there can be little certainty about this. It is unlikely that those who 'collected' or edited the Qur'ān under the caliph 'Uthmān had any material which they did not include; but some Muslims, usually from sectarian motives, have argued that passages from the Qur'ān have been lost. In general abrogated verses remain in the Qur'ān and are recited; but cf. comment on 22.52/1.

knowest thou not?: addressed to Muḥammad.

108/2 as Moses was questioned: the commentators say Moses was asked to show the people God or to produce a book revealed all at once.

109/3 restore you as unbelievers: many of the Jews made verbal attacks on Islam to induce the Muslims to abandon it.

111/05 – 121/15 Arguments against Jews, Christians and pagans

112/06 submits his will to God: Ar. *aslama wajha-hu li-llāh*; this is clearly related to *islām* or 'submission (to God)'. The phrase seems to be used in a general sense here, but out of such usages grew the technical use of 'Muslim' and 'Islam' for Muḥammad's followers and his religion.

113/07 The Jews say . . .: the point is that Jews and Christians deny one another's religion though they accept the same scriptures.

the ignorant: literally, those who do not know, probably referring to the 'pagan opposition' at Medina (cf. Watt, *Medina*, 178, and v. 78/3 above).

114/08 God's places of worship: Ar. *masājid*, the usual term for 'mosques'. The reference is uncertain. It can hardly be the pagan Meccans in this Medinan context. Jerusalem has been suggested, either previously under the Romans, or now under the Persians.

115/09 whithersoever you turn . . .: this is said to refer to the *qibla* (direction faced in prayer), and the story is told of some Muslims who on a very dark night could not find the right direction to face and wondered if their prayer was valid.

116/0 God has taken to Him a son: Ar. *walad*, which can also have the general sense of 'children', 'offspring'. The charge might be applied to Christians, to Jewish views of angels or of Ezra (cf. 9.30), or to the belief of pagans that their deities were angels or daughters of God. If verse 114/08 refers to pagans, then it is probable that they are referred to here too; and in general this seems to be the case where *walad* is used.

117/1 He but says to it, 'Be': no clumsy process of physical procreation is needed, since his mere word or *fiat* is immediately effective.

118/2 they that know not: presumably identical with 'the ignorant' cf. v. 113/07.

We have made clear the signs: the pagans doubtless wanted miracles, but Muḥammad is to reply that they have already received clear signs, presumably in the verses of the Qur'ān and its pointing to the signs in nature of God's power and goodness. The word *āyāt* means both 'signs' and 'verses'.

119/3 questioned: sc. at the Judgement and held responsible.

121/15 with true recitation: presumably refers to Jews and Christians and distinguishes those who have the true reading and true interpretation from those who in some way 'corrupt it'.

122/16 – 129/3 Appeal to the Jews; Abraham at Mecca

124/18 with certain words: notably the command to leave his country and to sacrifice his son.

leader: Ar. *imām*, the word later used for the leader of a religious community; but some commentators take it here as 'model' or 'example to be imitated'.

of my seed: sc. wilt thou make leaders or models?

125/19 the House: the Ka'ba or sanctuary of Mecca; as a centre of pilgrimage it was 'a place of visitation', and by the taboo on bloodshed in its neighbourhood it was a 'sanctuary' or place of security.

Abraham's station: a special spot in the precincts of the Ka'ba, but perhaps originally the whole site.

those that shall go about it: circumambulate the Ka'ba, as is still done.

those that cleave to it: who spend time in the precincts in meditation and devotion.

bow and prostrate: actions in Muslim prayer and worship.

126/0 a land secure: the sacred character of the area round the Ka'ba (or the whole of Mecca) and the prosperity of its people is ascribed to the prayer of Abraham.

127/1 raised up the foundations: there is no trace of any pre-Islamic legend connecting Abraham with the Ka'ba or with Mecca.

128/2 submissive . . . a nation submissive: Ar. *muslimīn . . . umma muslima*; the word *muslim* is here moving from the general to the special sense; cf. v. 112/06 above.

our holy rites: the pre-Islamic pilgrimage and other ceremonies retained in Islam are regarded as having been first introduced by Abraham at God's command.

129/3 a Messenger, one of them: there is perhaps some allusion to the word of Moses (*Deuteronomy*, 18.15), 'The Lord thy God will raise up unto thee a Prophet from the midst of thee, of thy brethren, like unto me'. The Qur'ān implies that this prayer is fulfilled in Muḥammad.

recite to them Thy signs: proclaim the revelation of the Qur'ān; cf. v. 118/2.

purify: Ar. *yuzakkī*, perhaps meaning 'purify by almsgiving' or 'appoint *zakāt* or legal alms'; cf. comment on 62.2.

130/24 – 141/35 The religion of Abraham

131/25 Surrender: or 'submit'; Ar. *aslim,* the imperative corresponding to the noun *islām.*

132/26 save in surrender: or 'save as Muslims'.

133/27 were you witnesses?: probably addressed to Jews and Christians to make the point that their religions were later than Abraham's.

we surrender: or 'we are submissive', Ar. *muslimūn.*

134/28 a nation that has passed away: or 'a community', Ar. *umma*; this is regarded as consisting of Abraham and his immediate successors, and as separate from the Jews and the Christians (founded by Moses and Jesus respectively). While a connection of the Jews and Christians with Abraham is not denied, the Qur'ān holds that they have deviated from the pure religion of Abraham.

there awaits them . . . : sc. in the future life the reward or punishment for what they have done.

135/29 the creed of Abraham: this implies that the religion of Islam is a restoration of the pure religion of Abraham, and therefore superior to Judaism and Christianity.

a man of pure faith: Ar. *ḥanīf*; this word has been much discussed (see art. by Watt in *EI*[2]); this usage has been developed in the Qur'ān to accord with the conception of 'the pure religion of Abraham'; while there were seekers for God in Arabia before Islam, there is no good evidence that any of these called himself a *ḥanīf.* Before the word 'Muslim' became a technical term, a follower of Muḥammad would call himself 'a believer' or 'a *ḥanīf*'. In 3.19/17 Ibn-Mas'ūd read *ḥanīfiyya* instead of *islām* (cf. Jeffery, *Materials,* 32), and this suggests that before Muḥammad's religion was called Islam it was called the Ḥanīfiyya or Ḥanīfite religion.

136/0 that which was given to Moses: the Torah or Old Testament as the foundation of Jewish religion.

we make no division: or 'distinction'; the Qur'ān regards all prophets (including patriarchs in *Genesis* and Jesus) as having received in essentials the same message; thus Muslims can claim to acknowledge all prophets alike whereas Christians (they say) refuse to acknowledge Muḥammad.

138/2 the baptism of God: Ar. *ṣibgha*, which means 'colouring by dipping into dye'. While the verse could possibly mean that God gives a man a certain colour when he serves Him, it is better to regard its interpretation as uncertain. It is doubtful if there is any reference to Christian baptism.

139/3 would you then dispute: 'you' addresses Jews and Christians, as 'us' refers to the Muslims.

140/34 they were Jews . . .: the conception of 'the religion of Abraham' is justified in part by the undeniable fact that Abraham was neither a Jew nor a Christian. The Jews may be defined as the descendants of Jacob or the followers of the revelation to Moses (in Islamic terms), but in either case Abraham is excluded. It is also worth remembering that, according to Biblical tradition, accepted by Muslim scholars, the Arabs are descended from Abraham through Ishmael.

conceals a testimony: viz. that Abraham was not a Jew.

142/36 – 152/47 The change of Qibla

142/36 the fools: Jews and other opponents, who tried to mock the Muslims because of the change to be mentioned.

the direction they were facing in their prayers: the Arabic word *qibla* signifies the direction faced in prayers; for many Christians this is the east. At first most Muslims seem to have faced Jerusalem, thus accepting the practice of the Jews of Medina.

In February 624, seventeen months after Muḥammad's arrival in Medina, a revelation came bidding the Muslims make the sanctuary of Mecca their *qibla*. This was an aspect of the so-called 'break with the Jews' (cf. Watt, *Prophet*, 112–18).

to God belong the East and the West: the implication is that no direction is inherently more suited than any other to be the direction of prayer.

143/37 a midmost nation: or 'community' (*umma*); various interpretations are given; e.g. intermediate between the strict legalism of the Jews and the indeterminateness of the Christians.

witnesses to the people: or 'against the people'; by 'people' (*nās*) may be meant all mankind, and if so, this marks the beginning of the belief in the universality of the Qur'ānic message.

143/38 and we did not appoint . . .: this gives a reason for the previous *qibla*, Jerusalem, but no verse exists prescribing Jerusalem as *qibla*.

though it were a grave thing: the change of *qibla* seemed a serious doubt-provoking matter, except to those who were convinced believers.

God would never leave your faith to waste: said to be revealed because some Muslims thought that previous prayers facing Jerusalem must have been vain; but the verse may be applied more generally.

144/39 turning thy face about in the heaven: traditionally taken as describing Muḥammad's desire to have some other *qibla* than Jerusalem; modern scholars have wondered if for a time there was no *qibla*.

turn thy face towards the Holy Mosque: this may be the actual revelation prescribing the change; the same words occur in 149/4 and 150/45.

145/0 thou are not a follower of their direction: the distinctive *qibla* separates Muslims from Jews and Christians, and implies that the inevitability of three communities has been accepted.

146/1 whom we have given . . . : the usual punctuation makes this a fresh sentence, viz.: 'those whom we have given the Book recognize . . .'.

recognize it: 'it' may refer to Muḥammad's message or to the supposed description of Muḥammad in the Torah; in the latter case the word might be translated 'him'. Cf. Ibn-Hishām, 353.

conceal the truth: the description of Muḥammad in the Torah.

148/3 direction: Ar. *wijha*, roughly equal to *qibla*; the thought is that worshippers of God are eminent through good works, not through a superior *qibla*.

150/45 turn your faces: what was first a command to Muḥammad is repeated for all Muslims.

any argument against you: some Muslims of Medina seem to have objected to Jerusalem as *qibla*; cf. the story of al-Barā' in Ibn-Hishām, 294 f.; Watt, *Medina*, 198 f.

151/46 of themselves: cf. v. 129/3.

152/47 ungrateful: Ar. *lā takfurū-nī*; or 'be not unbelievers', but the former, non-technical sense is more likely here.

153/48 – 167/2 Attitudes in bereavement and misfortune

154/49 those slain in God's way: that is, while fighting for the cause of God and the Muslims; this is said to have been revealed shortly after Badr.

156/1 Surely we belong to God and to Him we return: often repeated by Muslims in adversity.

158/3 Safa (Ṣafā) and Marwa: two low hills near the Ka'ba in Mecca. In pagan times there was a male idol on Ṣafā and a female on Marwa, and pilgrims ran back and forwards seven times. This verse legitimizes this ceremony of running (*sa'y*) for Muslim pilgrims, though the idols were of course destroyed. Traditionally the *sa'y* was held to commemorate Hagar's search for water when left here by Abraham.

the Visitation: that is, the *'umra* or lesser pilgrimage, which is confined to Mecca and can be made at any time of the year; the *ḥajj* or pilgrimage proper is made at only one specified time in the year and includes sites several miles from Mecca. The 'House' is the Ka'ba.

to circumambulate: this word is now used only of going round the Ka'ba, while the rite at Ṣafā and Marwa is known as the *sa'y* or 'running'.

volunteers: does voluntarily, without strict obligation.

159/4 those who conceal: the Jews.

show clearly: sc. what they concealed.

162/57 therein: in Hell, or under the curse.

164/59 signs: natural phenomena in which God's power is manifested; cf. v. 41/38, etc.

165/0 compeers: Ar. *andād*, 'rivals'; that is, deities alleged to be roughly on a footing of equality with God.

166/1 those that were followed: pagan deities, or else prophets whose followers disobeyed; cf. 5.116 (of Jesus).

168/3 – 182/78 Laws about food, retaliation and wills

168/3 lawful and good: these words must be interpreted in accordance with later Muslim practice.

170/65 such things as we found our fathers doing: if this applies to good laws, it might mean that some men objected to abandoning pagan food taboos; cf. 5.103/2. The verse might refer, however, to the worship of idols.

173/68 carrion: what is found dead or dies of itself; cf. *Leviticus*, 17.15.

blood: cf. *Genesis*, 9.4; *Leviticus*, 17.10–12; etc.

the flesh of swine: cf. *Leviticus*, 11.7; *Deuteronomy*, 14.8.

hallowed to other than God: sacrificed to idols; cf. *Acts*, 15.29. According to Islamic law animals for human consumption are slaughtered 'in the name of God', in much the same way as is done among orthodox Jews.

transgressing: i.e. deliberately in respect of eating something forbidden.

177/2 True piety: an important statement of the chief duties of Muslims in the early Medinan period; the part about belief is especially important and is often quoted.

traveller: Ar. *ibn as-sabīl*, literally 'the son of the way'; this follows the nomadic tradition of hospitality which was frequently a man's only hope of survival when travelling.

178/3 retaliation: the *lex talionis*, 'an eye for an eye, a tooth for a tooth, and a life for a life', is an effective way of keeping order in some types of primitive society (cf. *Leviticus*, 24.17–21); in the oldest forms the actual taking of a life is insisted on (cf. *Genesis*, 9.5 f.; *Numbers*, 35.31), and conservative Arabs in Muḥammad's time, when a man accepted a blood-wit of (usually a hundred) camels instead, taunted him with 'being content with milk instead of blood'. Islam accepted this practice of retaliation, which was still effective despite disputes about what constituted an equivalent in a given case, but encouraged men to accept a blood-wit of camels or money in place of an actual life.

is pardoned: that is, if blood is not insisted on, but a blood-wit accepted.

let the pursuing be honourable: that is, the next-of-kin in seeking the blood-wit, must act honourably or 'in accordance with accepted norms'.

in retaliation there is life: in that it restrains violence, it is an essential practice in a healthy society.

180/76 to make testament: questions of inheritance were a difficulty in the early Muslim community, probably because strong individuals tended to misuse and appropriate wealth that had hitherto been held communally. This verse is said to have been abrogated by 4.7/8–14/18, and by Islamic law a Muslim may not bequeath more than one-third of his property and may not bequeath it to anyone already entitled to a share.

honourably: Ar. *bi-l-ma'rūf*, probably meaning 'in accordance with accepted norms'.

181/77 changes it: sc. the testament, e.g. by trying to seize more than his due.

182/78 makes things right: that is, gets the testator during his lifetime to change a point on which he had been in error or unfair.

183/79 – 189/5 Fasting, etc

183/79 for those that were before you: the Jews, whose fast on the Day of Atonement was observed for a time by the Muslims in Medina.

184/0 for days numbered: the thirty days of the month of Ramaḍān, mentioned below.

a redemption: that is, to make up for deliberate non-observance of the fast.

volunteers good: said to mean doing more than the bare minimum in feeding the poor man.

185/1 wherein the Koran was sent down: since Muḥammad seems to have received revelations at all seasons of the year, this is usually interpreted of the sending down of the Qur'ān from the highest heaven to the lowest, or of the beginning of revelation; cf. sura 97.

Salvation: Ar. *furqān*; cf. comment on v. 53/0.

187/3 go in to your wives: fasting is taken to include abstinence from sexual intercourse.

what God has prescribed: interpreted as children.

eat and drink until . . .: the fast consists in abstinence from food, drink, smoking, and sexual intercourse from half an hour before dawn until half an hour after sunset, but there is no legal restriction on what is eaten during the night.

while you cleave to the mosques: Ar. *'ākifūn,* cf. v. 125/19; that is, while fulfilling a vow to spend a number of days in the mosque in prayer and meditation.

188/4 in vanity: in unscrupulous business practices, or perhaps in gambling.

proffer it: offer bribes.

189/5 new moons: presumably the questioners wanted to know whether they might observe some pagan rites; since the moon was the basis of Arab time-reckoning, this was retained by Islam; cf. 9.36 f.

to come to the houses from the backs: a pagan Arab practice observed by the Meccans at certain times; cf. *EI*², art. 'Ḥums'.

190/86 – 195/1 Fighting and the sacred months

190/86 fight in the way of God: fight for God's cause and that of the community of Muslims.

aggress not: do not be first to attack; but this is said to be abrogated; the command would be appropriate just before the expedition of al-Ḥudaybiya in March 628, or perhaps after it.

from where they expelled you: from Mecca.

191/87 persecution: presumably referring to the persecution of Muslims at Mecca by pagan Meccans. The extent of the persecution of Muslims at Mecca has been disputed by modern scholars; but the Qur'ān in this and similar passages is evidence that the Muslims felt they were being greatly persecuted.

the Holy Mosque: the whole area round the Ka'ba at Mecca was sacred territory, according to pre-Islamic ideas.

194/0 The holy month for the holy month; holy things demand retaliation: the idea is usually taken to be that non-observance of a taboo (of time, place, etc.) out of hostility may be countered by a similar non-observance of taboo. Though the taboos were originally matters of pagan religion, many were accepted by Islam.

195/1 expend in the way of God: make contributions of money or goods for the cause of the new religious community; these were probably needed chiefly to maintain at Medina the Emigrants from Mecca.

196/2 – 203/199 Pilgrimage to Mecca

196/2 The Pilgrimage: Ar. *ḥajj*; a pre-Islamic Arabian custom taken over by Islam with some modifications; the present verse is doubtless about the same time as the change of *qibla,* when the actual performance of the pilgrimage would be difficult at least for Muslims who had emigrated from Mecca. Cf. *EI*², art. 'Ḥadjdj'.

Visitation: cf. 158/3.

redemption: i.e. to make up for not shaving the head.

enjoys the Visitation until . . .: probably means performs the *'umra*, then stays on; but the passage is obscure.

197/3 in months well-known: the Pilgrimage rites all take place in *Dhū-l-ḥijja*, 'the pilgrimage month', but the two previous months are said to be included here, since the journey might be long.

198/4 press on from Arafat: 'Arafat is a rocky hill in the midst of a great valley some 22 km. from Mecca. The ritual act of 'standing at 'Arafāt' from midday to sunset on the ninth day of the Pilgrimage Month is reckoned the climax of the Pilgrimage, and nowadays there may be as many as half a million people present. From 'Arafāt, once the sun has set, the pilgrims 'press on' or hasten to Muzdalifa, 8 km. away.

the Holy Waymark: Ar. *al-mash'ar al-ḥarām*; now identified with 'the Mosque of the Sacred Grove' at Muzdalifa (Kamal, *Sacred Journey*, 84).

203/199 remember God during certain days: that is, the days of *tashrīq*, or of drying meat, when originally the flesh of the animals sacrificed at Minā was dried in the sun; all pilgrims are expected to spend at least two nights at Minā after the night of the tenth (*Sacred Journey*, 90).

204/0 – 219/7 Various matters

204/0 some men there are: apparently a man or men who raided farms, but nothing further is known.

208/4 enter the peace: Ar. *as-salm*; usually interpreted as *the peace of God* with the implication of *islām* or submission to him.

213/09 the people were one nation: or 'mankind were one (religious) community' (*umma*).

were at variance upon it . . . being insolent: as in the Biblical story of the tower of Babel, the divisions among mankind are here regarded as due to insolence, but the primary reference is probably to religious disputes between Jews and Christians.

214/0 without there had come upon you . . .: may be addressed to Medinan Muslims to remind them they must suffer as the original Muslims in Mecca suffered.

216/2 Prescribed for you is fighting . . .: the Muslims of Medina had pledged themselves to defend Muḥammad from any attack, but some were alarmed as they saw warfare spreading, and found it 'hateful'; but warfare was necessary for the establishing of Islam.

217/4 the holy month: cf. comment on v. 194/0.

218/5 those who emigrate: sc. from Mecca to Medina to join Muḥammad; they also 'struggle in God's way' or fight.

219/6 wine: taken to include all intoxicating drinks.

arrow-shuffling: Ar. *maysir,* a game in which lots were drawn by arrows to decide who would have the best parts of a camel which was to be slaughtered and who would pay for it; may be taken to include all gambling.

219/7 the abundance: Ar. *'afw,* meaning what is redundant and what one can spare.

220/18 – 237/8 Marriage and family affairs

220/19 intermix: probably refers to making use of their property in business operations.

221/0 idolatresses—idolaters: marriage between Muslins and pagans is absolutely forbidden.

223 *tillage:* a development of the primitive metaphor which compares sexual intercourse with the sowing of seed, and speaks of children as the fruit of the womb.

as you wish: the Arabic *annā*, 'as', may refer to time or manner; those who take it in the second sense say it refers to the various postures in intercourse, but that 'unnatural' practices are excluded by the words 'as God has commanded you' in the previous verse.

forward for your souls: often interpreted as uttering a pious phrase before intercourse.

224 *Do not make God a hindrance:* by taking such oaths as would hinder the performance of the various duties.

226 *forswear:* take an oath to abstain from intercourse; after the 'wait of four months' the man must decide either to restore the marriage or divorce the woman.

228 *wait by themselves for three periods:* a woman who is divorced may not marry another man until after an *'idda* or waiting-period of three menstrual periods or, if she prove to be pregnant, until after the birth of the child. The next clause says it is unlawful to hide the fact of pregnancy.

Women have such honourable rights as obligations: Literally 'have rights similar to their duties according to what is honourable (or reputable or customary)'; this is sometimes said to mean that both parties should keep the way open for reconciliation.

229 *Divorce is twice:* the interpretation is that a man may divorce a woman twice and remarry her; but if he divorces her a third time, it is not lawful for them to remarry until she has been married to another man and been divorced by him (v. 230).

what you have given them: the dowry given by the man to the woman; when divorced by repudiation (*ṭalāq*) she retains this; but—so the rest of the verse seems to mean—if inability to give her the dowry would mean the continuation of an impossible marriage, she may remit all or part.

to redeem herself: to gain her freedom.

231 *do not retain them by force:* e.g. by insisting on the surrender of part of the dowry.

232 *from marrying their husbands:* usually taken to mean that the relatives should not oppose remarriage to the former husband, but might refer to opposition by the former husband to another husband.

233 *Mothers:* that is, after divorce; maintenance must be paid for this period.

shall not be pressed: these rules must not be applied oppressively and unreasonably.

nursing: it was common for wealthy people to have a wet-nurse; Muḥammad was sent to one in the desert.

234 *four months and ten nights:* the text has only 'ten' and 'days' is usually supplied; this wait ensures that the widow is not pregnant. This verse abrogates the 'year' mentioned in verse 240/1.

235 *the proposal:* that is, of marriage to widows during the period of four months and ten days (the 'book' mentioned below).

237/8 *in whose hand is the knot of marriage:* the bridegroom, or, as is more likely, the woman's guardian, who acts for her in the legal aspects.

238/9 – 245/6 Danger and death

238/9 *the middle prayer:* usually taken as the afternoon prayer (*'aṣr*), but the five times of prayer are not explicitly mentioned in the Qur'ān.

239/40 in fear: of attacks by enemies, etc.; in such cases the ritual prayer may be performed walking or riding.

240/1 year: this was abrogated by verse 234.

241/2 for divorced women: usually taken as referring to testamentary provision for them during their waiting period.

243/4 those who went forth: said to be Israelites who fled to avoid pestilence or war, but were struck dead by God, though later restored to life by the prophet Ezekiel; the inevitability of death at a particular time is a common theme in pre-Islamic poetry.

245/6 lend: by contributing to God's cause.

246/7 – 252/3 The story of Saul, Goliath and David

246/7 a Prophet: i.e. Samuel, cf. *I Samuel*, 8.

who have been expelled: there is a clear parallel to the situation of the Emigrants in Medina.

248/9 the Ark: Ar. at-Tābūt.

Shechina: the Ar. *sakīna* appears to be a rendering of this Hebrew word, meaning God's glory; but in the five other places in the Qur'ān where it is used the meaning 'assurance' fits best; here it is rather some visible object, deliberately left vague. Some of the many interpretations of Muslim scholars are discussed by Ignaz Goldziher, *Abhandlungen zur arabischen Philologie*, i. 177–204 (Leiden, 1896).

249/50 him who scoops up: cf. the story of Gideon, *Judges*, 7.4–7.

251/2 David slew Goliath: cf. 1 *Samuel*, 17.

252/3 – 254/5 Certainty of Muhammad's prophethood and that of Jesus; contributions

253/4 those who came after him: usual reading 'after them'; the reference is to the disputes between Jews and Christians.

255/6 – 257/9 God's sublimity and support of believers

255/6 God: this is the 'throne verse', greatly admired by Muslims and frequently recited; the throne (*kursī*, used only here and of Solomon in 38.34/3) is the actual seat, whereas the *'arsh* (7.54/2, etc.) is the whole structure, perhaps including platform and canopy; there have been many mystical interpretations of both concepts.

256/7 idols: Ar. *Ṭāghūt* (from Ethiopic) sometimes treated as a proper name.

258/60 – 260/2 Disputes about resurrection

258/60 him who disputed: traditionally identified with Nimrod (*Genesis*, 10.8–10), who is supposed to have been king of Abraham's native land.

259/61 he who passed by: said to be Ezra ('Uzayr).

260/1 four birds: cf. *Genesis*, 15.9.

261/3 – 274/5 Contributions and alms

262/4 reproach and injury: that is, remind him that he is indebted to them, and expose his poverty to his hurt.

266/8 seed: children.

273/4 restrained: may mean *either* that poverty keeps them from joining campaigns through lack of armour and a mount, *or* that because they are engaged on campaigns they are unable to make trading journeys to earn a living.

275/6 – 284 Prohibition of usury; treatment of debtors

275/6 usury: literally 'increase'; there continues to be argument about what precisely is forbidden, though the standard interpretation has been the lending of money on interest.

of the touch: that is, by touching, the reference being to demoniac possession and convulsions.

trafficking: probably trading by bargaining.

280 freewill offerings: the idea seems to be that what was lent to the man now in difficulties should be made an outright gift; this would apply especially if the loans were made to needy Emigrants shortly after the Hijra.

285 f. Profession and prayer of the believers

286 charges . . . to its capacity: i.e. requires of no one more than he is able to perform.

earned, merited: good and bad deeds respectively; Ar. *kasabat, iktasabat*; the former word was used by Ash'arite theologians to describe a man's relation to his act when it is regarded as primarily God's doing; 'God creates the act, man appropriates it (*kasaba*)'.

3
THE HOUSE OF IMRAN
Āl 'Imrān

Most of this sura belongs to the second and third years of the Hijra, much of it being connected with events surrounding the battle of Uḥud in March 625 (x. 3 A.H.). An account of the battle will be found in *Medina*, 21–9, *Prophet*, 135–44. The earlier part contains material relevant to the dispute with the Jews.

1 – 9/7 The Book

3/2 the Book: the totality of the revelations which had come to Muḥammad, and which had not at first been regarded as parts of a whole; cf. Watt and Bell, *Introduction*, 141–4.

confirming what was before it: that is, the Qur'ānic revelation, being the same in essentials as previous revelations, confirms the Jewish revelation made to Moses in the Torah and the Christian revelation made to Jesus in the Gospel. The Torah (Hebrew for 'law' or 'instruction') is properly the Books of Moses or Pentateuch, but, as the revealed scripture of the Jews, may be said to correspond to the (Christian) Old Testament. Similarly the Gospel (Ar. Injīl) is assumed to be a single book, and, as the scripture of the Christians, may stand for the whole New Testament.

Salvation: cf. 2.53/0; perhaps here means the victory of Badr.

7/5 Essence: literally 'mother' (*umm*).

ambiguous: this is the usual interpretation of *mutashābihāt*, though it could mean 'resembling one another'.

swerving: an inclination to leave the straight path.

10/8 – 17/15 Fate of unbelievers and believers

13/11 two companies: the Muslims and the pagan Meccans who met at the battle of Badr.

they saw them: usually taken to mean that the unbelievers saw the believers twice as many as themselves (though the unbelievers were more numerous). By causing this false appearance God increased the fear of the pagans and so helped the believers.

17/15 at the daybreak: perhaps a reference to the time of the first of the five daily prayers.

18/16 – 20/19 Islam

18/16 and the angels: sc. also bear witness.

19/17 Islam: the word here is not simply a name, but has its primary connotation of 'surrender' as in verse 20/18.

the knowledge: given by revelation; the reference is to disputes between Jews and Christians after the revelation to Jesus.

20/18 and whosoever follows me: sc. has also surrendered.

20/19 those given the Book: the Jews (of Medina).

the common folk: Ar. *ummiyyīn*, cf. 2.78/3; the reference here might be to the Arabs who were subordinate to the Jews and did not at first become Muslims.

21/0 – 27/6 Attacks on the Jews

21/0 slay the Prophets: a common accusation against the Jews.

23/2 a portion of the Book: implying that some matters at least of detail were not present in the revelation to the Jews; but some merely say the Jews of Medina had a defective knowledge of their scripture.

called to the Book: one of the stories given in explanation is that, when Muḥammad remarked to some Jews that he was of the religion of Abraham, and they replied that Abraham was a Jew, he challenged them to look at their scriptures and they refused; cf. v. 93/87. (For Abraham see Index.)

24/3 The Fire shall not touch us: cf. 2.80/74.

26/5 givest the Kingdom: if this was originally connected with the preceding verses, it could mean that God has taken power from the Jews of Medina (or in general) and given it to the Muslims.

27/6 providest: with the necessaries of life.

28/7 – 32/29 Believers to avoid unbelievers and follow Muḥammad

28/7 for friends: or allies, so that there is mutual protection; Islam was to replace even the solidarity of kinship.

unless you have a fear of them: (Ar. *tattaqū tuqayya*); permits those in special circumstances, e.g. those dependent on unbelievers, to have official relationships; the verse was later used to justify *taqiyya*, verbal denial of Islam when in danger of one's life.

33/0 – 41/36 Birth and nurture of Mary; Zachariah

33/0 House of Imran: i.e. the Biblical Amram, father of Moses (*Exodus*, 6.20).

36/1 a female: who could not be dedicated to temple service as vowed; but special arrangements were made.

Mary: Ar. Maryam. There is apparent confusion with Miriam, sister of Moses. Muslim commentators explain this in various ways, e.g. by holding there were two persons called 'Imrān. It is also possible that the confusion was present in the mind of the Arabs of Medina, and that it was not part of the purpose of the Qur'ān to correct this confusion; cf. 19.28/9.

the accursed Satan: or 'Satan the stoned', Ar. *rajīm*. It is said that the devil tempted Abraham to disobey God by not sacrificing his son, and that Abraham drove the devil away by throwing stones. There might be a suggestion of the doctrine of the immaculate conception.

37/2 Sanctuary: Ar. *miḥrāb*, a word of varied meaning (cf. C. E. Padwick, *Muslim Devotions*, London, 1961, 57–9), but the above rendering is probably best here. Later Muslim tradition spoke of Zachariah building a chamber for Mary in the temple precinct. There seems to be no Christian precedent for the story.

38/3 Zachariah prayed: cf. *Luke*, 1.5–20.

39/4 shall confirm a Word of God: or 'from God'; presumably referring, as the commentator al-Bayḍāwī notes, to Jesus who is called 'a word from God' in verse 45/0.

chaste: ascetic, abstemious in all things.

41/36 at evening and dawn: the times of the fifth and first of the Muslim daily prayers; cf. also *Psalms*, 55.17.

42/37 – 48/3 The Annunciation to Mary

42/37 the angels said: cf. *Luke,* 1.26–38.

45/0 near stationed: Ar. *min al-muqarrabīn,* 'of those brought near', a word often applied to angels and cognate with 'cherubim'.

46/1 in the cradle: cf. sura 19.29/30–33/4.

and of age: when adult; but some Muslim commentators take this of his second coming.

49/3 – 63/56 Jesus, his apostles and opponents

49/3 to be a Messenger: grammatically this appears to be part of what the angel said to Mary, but in fact it is a description of the work of Jesus.

the likeness of a bird: in the apocryphal Gospel of the Infancy Jesus as a child made beasts and birds of clay, and then made them come alive. In the Qur'ān the giving of life to the clay bird becomes a 'sign' of his prophethood.

by the leave of God: that is, the miracle is not performed by Jesus through any power of his own.

52/45 helpers: Ar. *anṣār,* the word used of the Medinan Muslims in contrast to the Meccan 'Emigrants' to Medina.

the Apostles: Ar. Ḥawāriyyūn, a special word, derived from Ethiopic, used only for the twelve apostles of Jesus.

our submission: Ar. *bi-an-nā muslimūn,* 'that we are submitting or surrendering or Muslims'; believers in previous revelations (especially Jewish and Christian), are regarded as Muslims, since the revelations are in principle the same.

54/47 they devised: that is, Jesus' opponents plotted against him; what God devised in return was, according to Muslim scholars, the substitution for Jesus of a phantom or of some other person (such as Judas); cf. sura 4.157/6.

55/48 will raise thee: many Muslim scholars believe that God took Jesus to heaven without his previous death, and then hold that the words 'will take thee to Me' refer to his death on the occasion of his second coming; the word 'raise' is also associated with the ascension (*Acts*, 1.6–12).

will set thy followers above the unbelievers: often interpreted to mean that Christians and Muslims (as following Jesus as a prophet) will be politically superior to the Jews.

59/2 as Adam's likeness: both were created by God's word 'Be', Adam from dust and Jesus in the womb of Mary.

61/54 lay God's curse: in Arabia the invoking of a calamity on oneself and one's family if one was speaking falsely was regarded as a kind of evidence. The commentators tell of an incident known as the *mubāhala* or 'mutual cursing' when Muḥammad, in defence of his belief about Jesus, was prepared to call down destruction on himself, his daughter Fāṭima and her husband 'Alī, and their children al-Ḥasan and al-Ḥusayn. Cf. 24.7.

64/57 – 71/64 Appeal to the Jews; Abraham not one

64/57 a word common: that is, to doctrines held in common by Jews and Muslims.

associate not aught with him: that is, ascribe divinity to some other being.

67/0 pure of faith: Ar. *ḥanīf*; cf. comment on 2.135/29.

71/64 conceal the truth: usually implies that the Jews concealed prophecies foretelling Muḥammad.

72/65 – 85/79 Criticisms of the Jews

72/65 disbelieve at the end of it: the Jews apparently hoped, by first saying they believed and then expressing doubt, that they would detach some Muslims from their belief.

75/69 no way over us: nothing obligatory for us.

as to the common people: Ar. *ummiyyīn*; here 'in respect of the non-Jews (gentiles)'.

77/1 sell God's covenant and their oaths: probably means make false oaths.

78/2 twist their tongues: perhaps refers to play on words; the assertion 'it is from God' may refer to Jewish oral law; cf. 2.79/3.

79/3 servants to me: this might refer to a Christian claim that Jesus had commanded them to worship him. It may also be noted that Muḥammad did not make his claim to political authority rest solely on his prophethood.

masters: or 'rabbis', Ar. *rabbaniyyīn*; the Arabic word for 'lord' is *rabb*.

81/75 took compact with the Prophets: God is said in this way to have assembled the souls of the prophets, born and unborn, at Sinai when the Torah was given to Moses; this Talmudic story is here used to suggest that the Jews should accept Muḥammad.

85/79 Islam: or 'surrender to God'; the name is applicable to previous revelations according to Muslim ideas.

86/0 – 101/96 Exhortations to hesitant believers

86/0 have disbelieved after they believed: this marks the seriousness of apostasy, though a loophole is made by 89/3; it may refer to Jews disbelieving in Jesus; cf. 106/2.

93/87 all food was lawful: this is said to refer to disputes between Muḥammad and the Jews about the consuming of the milk and flesh of camels; Jacob was said to have abstained from it voluntarily.

96/0 Bekka: another form of 'Mecca'; in the next verse pilgrimage to the Kaʻba is regarded as a duty to God. This revelation was presumably before the battle of Badr, when some Muslims were presumably still able to visit Mecca. It is said to be exalting Mecca above Jerusalem after the change of Qibla.

97/1 insecurity: because the sacredness of it made violence taboo.

99/4 bar from God's way: or 'keep back from'; this is said to refer to attempts by a Jew, Sha's ibn-Qays, to sow dissension among the Muslims of Medina by speaking of the battle of Buʻāth, a few years before the Hijra, when they had fought one another.

102/97 – 117/3 Address to believers before Uḥud

102/97 save in surrender: if you have to die (*sc.* in the expected fighting), see that you remain faithfully surrendered to God (*muslimūn*).

103/98 enemies: perhaps referring to the battle of Buʻāth.

105/01 fell into variance: probably meaning Jews (and perhaps also Christians): Jews also may be accused of disbelieving after believing, perhaps because they disbelieved Jesus.

110/06 the best nation: or 'community', addressed to the believers in Medina.

believed: that is, in Muḥammad's revelation.

110/07 will not harm you: this implies that the Muslims were apprehensive lest some of the Jews turned against them.

if they fight with [against] you: this shows that even an armed attack was contemplated; such a fear would be specially significant if the passage was revealed before the battle of Uḥud; if it was revealed immediately after, then the Muslims must have been expecting trouble from an-Naḍīr.

112/08 in a bond of God . . . of the people: this makes an exception of those Jews who were in some form of alliance with Muḥammad ('bond of God'; cf. references to Jews in the Constitution of Medina—*Medina,* 221–5) or had continued a pre-Islamic alliance with a clan or tribe of Muslim Arabs in Medina.

poverty: presumably through hostile acts by the Muslims.

113/09 a nation upstanding: or 'a community steadfast'; said to refer to Jewish converts to Islam, though only a few names are known, which hardly justifies 'nation' or 'community'; for a time the Muslims practised meditation by night (cf. sura 73); the words 'bowing themselves' refer to the prostration (*sujūd*) in the ritual prayers (cf. v. 43/38 above).

117/3 of that they expend: perhaps refers to the 'contributions' of Hypocrites.

118/4 – 120/16 Breaking off relations

118/4 intimates: Ar. *biṭāna*; apparently denotes a definite relationship, since it is mentioned in the Constitution, but the precise nature is unknown; cf. *Medina,* 224 n.

119/5 all of it: that is, what was revealed to Moses and Jesus as well as what was revealed to Muḥammad, in contrast to the Jews who did not accept Muḥammad's revelation; this makes it likely the passage refers to Jews.

121/17 – 129/4 Comments on the battle of Uḥud

121/17 people: Ar. *ahl,* 'family'.

lodge . . . in their pitches: assign their battle positions on the hill of Uḥud; the Muslims had marched out to the hill under cover of darkness.

122/18 two parties: said to be the clans of Salima and Ḥāritha, who had been disheartened by the words of 'Abd-Allāh ibn-Ubayy, leader of the Hypocrites.

123/19 utterly abject: probably implies that they were inferior in number.

126/2 wrought this: made this announcement through Muḥammad.

127/2 might cut off a part: at the beginning of the battle the Meccan infantry advanced towards the hill and were repulsed with heavy losses.

130/25 – 138/2 Prohibition of usury, etc

130/25 usury: presumably refers to some way of taking advantage of the critical circumstances in Medina at the time of the battle of Uḥud.

134/28 expend in almsgiving: Ar. *yunfiqūn,* 'contribute', is the opposite of 'usury' and may mean giving to needy Muslims, either directly or through Muḥammad.

139/3 – 151/44 Address after Uḥud

139/3 you shall be the upper ones: you believers will ultimately prevail.

140/34 if a wound touches you: or 'has touched you'; this almost certainly refers to the Muslim losses at Uḥud, and would mean that the passage was revealed after the battle; Bell thinks the whole passage was revealed before the battle, but this is less likely.

a like wound: the Meccans had lost fully as many at Badr.

such days we deal out in turn: ups and downs are to be expected in war; before Islam the Arabs referred to the battle of K as 'the day of K'.

witnesses: probably in the sense of 'martyrs'; the Greek *martyres* means 'witnesses'.

147/37 longing for death: some Muslims not present at Badr are said to have longed for an opportunity of gaining the honour of martyrdom, but to have been dismayed at the actual sight of the large Meccan army.

144/38 if he should die: this seems intended to allay anxiety after Muḥammad had been wounded; for a short time word got about that he had been killed.

145/39 at an appointed time: assurance is given by the pre-Islamic belief that the date of a man's death (his term—*ajal*) is fixed, though the bringing about of death is asserted to be under God's control.

146/0 with whom: along with whom.

151/44 cast . . . terror: this is often taken to refer to the retreat of the Meccans from Medina though they had had the better of the fighting at Uḥud.

152/45 – 155/49 Explanation of the discomfiture

152/45: God has been true: after the battle many Muslims were perturbed at the loss of life, and wondered whether they were mistaken in thinking God had supported them: cf. 154/48. The present passage aims at setting their doubts at rest. God did indeed fulfil his promise, in that for a time they had the upper hand and destroyed many of the Meccan infantry.

lost heart: perhaps rather 'became slack'; the usual story is that they started to think of the booty and to break order.

quarrelled about the matter: an obscure phrase; it could perhaps mean that they disputed whether to continue the pursuit or to halt for plunder.

were rebellious: the archers, stationed to guard the flank, are said to have left their places to make for the booty; this gave the Meccans the opportunity to launch a flanking cavalry attack which threw the Muslims into confusion and caused most of their casualties.

that you longed for: the booty in the Meccan camp; or victory.

152/46 He turned you: in flight and confusion.

153/47 going up: presumably climbing the hill of Uḥud, but going farther than necessary.

calling you in your rear: trying to reform his men on the lower slopes where they were already safe from the cavalry.

what escaped you: booty not taken.

154/48 a slumber: it is usually said that this was refreshing sleep which restored the vigour of those who had kept beside Muḥammad.

pagan thoughts: literally, thoughts of the *jāhiliyya* or pre-Islamic period; that is, doubts about God's control of events.

if we had had a part in the affair: probably means 'if our advice had been followed and we had not gone out to battle'; a number of Muslims had advised this and Muḥammad had at first favoured this course.

155/49 those . . . who turned away: 'Abd-Allāh ibn-Ubayy and his supporters; though here pardoned they were later denounced as Hypocrites.

earned: for some sin they had committed.

156/0 – 164/58 Reassurance after Uḥud

156/0 when they journey ...: 'for trade' is probably implied, just as 'expeditions' are raids for booty.

an anguish: acceptance of the fixity of the day of death removes anxiety and gives a certain serenity, even to the pagan Arab; the rest of this verse and the following one show the Muslim that he has greater cause for assurance.

159/3 gentle: addressed to Muḥammad personally, but the exact reference is not clear; perhaps it was his attitude to the Hypocrites.

161/55 fraudulent: some accusation of unfair treatment had been made against Muḥammad; it is said, but is not likely, that the archers left their places because they supposed they would not be given a share of the booty.

164/58 from themselves: cf. 2.129/3.

165/59 – 175/69 Purpose of the reverse

165/59 an affliction: the loss of life at Uḥud.

visited twice over: or 'caused twice over'; usually said to mean they had killed as many at Badr as they had lost at Uḥud, and in addition had taken as many prisoners.

from your own selves: because of disobedience.

166/0 that He might know: the purpose of the reverse is to distinguish between true believers and Hypocrites; this appears to be a little later than the previous verse pardoning the Hypocrites (if it has been correctly interpreted). The word 'Hypocrites' (*munāfiqūn*) is probably used for the first time here.

if only we knew how to fight: sc. successfully and not simply be killed; this, the usual interpretation, is required by the context; it is suggested in the next verse that their assertion that the decision to fight was disastrous was only an excuse.

172/66 those who answered: those who stood firm with Muḥammad after the cavalry charge had thrown the Muslims into confusion.

176/0 – 180/75 Unbelievers warned

176/0 that vie . . . in unbelief: perhaps the Hypocrites.

178/2 the unbelievers: probably this refers to opponents at Medina; but it would also be appropriate to the Meccans; in either case 'indulgence' means 'respite from immediate punishment'.

179/3 the state: of living mixed up with unbelievers; but He will distinguish the two.

180/75 those who are niggardly: probably not a general statement, but having particular reference to those who failed to 'contribute' before Uḥud.

181/76 – 188/5 Arguments with Jews

181/76 God is poor: this is probably an inference from the Qur'ānic appeals to 'lend to God a good loan' (73.20) and the like; cf. Ibn-Hishām, 388 f.

their slaying the Prophets: shows Jews are addressed.

183/79 a sacrifice devoured by fire: perhaps based on the story of Elijah and the prophets of Baal (1 *Kings*, 18.17–46).

185/2 removed from the Fire: usually taken to mean 'kept far from Hell'.

187/4 sold it: probably means that for bribes or out of self-interest they concealed the prophecies of Muḥammad supposed to be in their scripture.

189/6 – 200 God's majesty and the sure hope of believers

195/4 those who emigrated: the Emigrants from Mecca to Medina; it is not clear whether the following words 'were expelled from their habitations' refer simply to the Emigrants or distinguishes certain persons expelled from the voluntary Emigrants.

199/8 some there are: cf. v. 113/09.

4
THE WOMEN
An-nisā'

Much of this sura appears to have been revealed between the battle of Uḥud and the siege of Medina, but some passages, especially those referring to the Jews, are probably before Uḥud.

1 – 6/7 Treatment of orphans; marriage

1 *by whom you demand:* that is, when you say 'I adjure you by God'.

the wombs: that is, fear or respect blood-relationship, probably as used in oaths or adjurations.

2 *exchange the corrupt:* by giving the orphans their share from what was of poorest quality.

devour not their property: much property had hitherto been communal, and it was easy for an unscrupulous man to treat communal property as his own individual property.

3 *will not act justly towards the orphans:* there were still many traces of polyandry and similar practices at Medina (cf. *Medina*, 373–88); the unjust treatment of girl orphans presumably consisted in keeping them 'polyandrous' and so subject not to any husband but to the guardian, who doubtless could make some profit from this arrangement. The passage is said to have been revealed after the death of many male Muslims at the battle of Uḥud.

marry . . . two, three, four: the point is presumably that if each Muslim marries several wives, no girl orphans need be left in the inferior 'polyandrous' condition; it is to be noted that this verse, on which the permission for a Muslim to have four wives is based, does not restrict a previous unlimited polyandry.

will not be equitable: some modern Muslims argue that, since no man can be impartial between several women, this virtually prescribes monogamy.

what your right hands own: slave-girls; a Muslim could have any number of slave-concubines in addition to the four legal wives.

4/3 dowries: Ar. *ṣaduqāt,* not the usual *mahr*; the precise meaning here is thus uncertain; perhaps 'morning-gift'.

6/5 test well the orphans: that is, girl orphans, both as regards acting responsibly and in respect of physical maturity.

7/8 – 14/18 Rules for inheritance

The basic principle of the Islamic law of inheritance is that most of the property of a man or woman must be divided in fixed proportions among the closest relatives. This was a wise provision in the circumstances of the time—a period of transition from communal to individual property. The rules are complex, and the numerous possibilities are discussed at length in manuals of Islamic law.

12/14 after any bequest: bequests are not normally allowed to the relatives entitled to a share; and the total amount of bequests must not exceed one-third of the estate.

15/19 – 28/32 Rules about marriage and marital offences

15/19 indecency: now interpreted by adultery and fornication, but probably referred originally to practices connected with polyandry.

16/20 two of you: often interpreted of two males; but more probably it was something connected with polyandry.

19/23 to inherit women: it was an old Semitic custom for a woman, on the death of her husband, to become the wife of his eldest son (by another woman cf. v. 22/6 below) or of some other close relative; cf. *Ruth*, 3.12; *Mark*, 12.18–25; *Deuteronomy*, 25.5–10.

debar them: this is said to mean debarring a wife from divorce and remarriage to get her to renounce part of the dowry given to her.

20/24 exchange a wife: by divorce and remarriage.

23/7 forbidden to you . . .: the forbidden degrees, within which marriage would be incestuous.

your mothers who have given suck . . . your suckling sisters: the 'milk-relationship' created by suckling was and is regarded as being as close as a blood-relationship; Muslim mothers sometimes deliberately exchange sucklings for a short time in order to create milk-relationships; perhaps the aim is to increase the opportunities of men and women mixing—an important consideration where the sexes are segregated.

24/8 wedded women: Ar. *muḥṣināt* or *muḥṣanāt*, 'keeping themselves or kept inviolable'; keeping themselves to one man at a time; cf. *Medina*, 389–92, and 24.23 below.

beyond all that: this is said originally to have permitted *mut'a* or temporary marriage.

in wedlock and not in licence: Ar. *muḥṣinīn ghayr musāfiḥīn*, presumably meaning 'provided that during the union they have intercourse only with you and not (in polyandric fashion) with other men'.

29/33 – 33/7 Gambling; murder; covetousness

29/33 in vanity: gambling.

trading: this is perhaps meant to allow a speculative element in trading, such as buying crops before they are ripe.

34/8 – 42/5 Men's control of women and care for others

34/8 that they have expended: sc. in maintaining their wives.

guarding the secret for God's guarding: usually taken as 'guarding themselves and their husband's property, in return for God's guarding them'.

banish: have no marital relations.

37/41 bounty: said to be the knowledge of Muḥammad being named as a prophet; but it is more likely to mean material wealth.

39/43 expended: sc. contributed to the cause of the Muslims.

43/6 Preparation for worship

wholesome dust: when water is not available ablutions may be performed with clean dry sand.

44/7 – 57/60 Criticisms of the Jews

44/7 desiring that you should also err: the Jews are said to have tried to get the Muslims to stop contributing money, as well as throwing doubts on Muḥammad's prophethood.

46/8 pervert words from their meanings: this is illustrated by the following lines, explained in the notes on 2.93/87 and 104/98.

47/50 Sabbath-men: cf. 2.65/1.

48/51 less than that He forgives: the one unforgivable sin is *shirk*, associating other beings with God in worship.

49/52 purify themselves: assert that they are pure or justified; Jews primarily are meant because of their belief in themselves as a Chosen People.

51/4 believing in demons and idols: this verse is said to refer to an incident during the preparations for the siege of Medina; some Jewish rabbis were in Mecca and in reply to a question said the Meccans' religion was better than Muḥammad's (Ibn-Hishām, 391).

demons: Ar. Jibt, perhaps a proper name; for 'idols' (Ṭāghūt) cf. 2.256/7.

54/7 a mighty kingdom: the commentators refer this to the kingdom of David and Solomon, but it might rather be the Byzantine empire.

55/8 bar from it: the revelation; or 'from him', Muḥammad.

58/61 – 70/72 Trusts; referring of disputes to Muḥammad

58/61 to deliver trusts: maintaining a trust was a pagan Arab virtue; it is said the verse applied in the first place to the key of the Ka'ba at the conquest of Mecca.

59/62 refer it to God and the Messenger: the Constitution of Medina (§§23,42) (Watt, *Medina*, 221–5) says disputes are to be so referred, but the repetition of verses like the present suggests that the regulation was not observed for several years; cf. 42.10/8. Cf. also verse 65/8 below.

60/3 hast thou not regarded ...: this must refer to some particular incident, but none of the stories told corresponds exactly to the passage.

66/9 Slay yourselves: said to be something comparable to the punishment of the Israelites after the worship of the calf. Perhaps it means rather 'Go on expeditions in which you may lose your life', and in that case 'Leave your habitations' might mean 'Make the Hijra'; cf. 100/1.

71/3 – 81/3 Encouragement to fight

71/3 take your precautions: might mean to make preparations for defence as for an expedition; there is no clear account of the occasion when this passage was revealed, but it fits the time just before the second expedition to Badr (a year after Uḥud) when no fighting in fact took place.

72/4 are dilatory: fall behind, or fail to be ready in time for the expedition.

73/5 any affection: so that he could have joined you had he wanted, and indeed ought to have joined you.

74/6 sell the present life: do not hesitate to risk their lives.

75/7 being abased: Ar. *mustaḍ'afīn*, literally 'regarded as weak'. The reference is to the Muslims who were kept in Mecca ('this city') by their relatives.

76/8 fight in the idols' way: or 'way of Ṭāghūt'; cf. story that Abū-Sufyān, the Meccan leader, took the idols al-Lāt and al-'Uzzā with him to the battle of Uḥud.

77/9 rest your hands: from violence or fighting; the people described are ready to follow Muḥammad when no risk of life is involved.

a near term: the time of our natural death, which is near in any case.

78/80 raised-up towers: the people of Medina had towers or forts to which they could retire and be safe from attack; many had wanted to retire to these instead of marching out to Uḥud; the verse expresses the prevailing Arab belief that the day of death was ineluctably fixed.

79/81 whatever good visits thee: 'thee' could be understood of man in general; even if taken of Muḥammad, it must be of general application.

82/4 – 87/9 Various matters

83/5 they broadcast it: ill-wishers in Medina divulge secrets about military movements to Muḥammad's enemies, and also spread rumours which alarm his followers.

86/8 greet with a fairer than it, or return it: when a Muslim receives the greeting 'Peace be with you', he replies 'And with you peace' or he may say 'Peace be with you and God's mercy and blessing'.

88/90 – 91/3 Hesitant supporters

This passage apparently refers to a group of incidents which have been largely forgotten. The 'hypocrites' in 88/90 do not appear to be 'Abd-Allāh ibn-Ubayy and his followers, since the mention of them 'emigrating' in 89/91 implies that they are not in Medina. The most likely stories are those which assert that the reference is to nomadic tribes. The presumption is that these had shown interest in Islam and then turned back. They are not to be treated as allies unless they go to 'a people joined with you by a compact' (*sc.* allies) or come to Medina.

90/2 with breasts constricted: their situation is difficult, since they must either fight Muḥammad or fight their own tribe.

authority over you: that is, would have given them dominion over you or would have caused them to prevail over you.

assigns not any way: does not permit you to attack them.

91/3 secure from you: that is, not liable to be attacked either by you or by their own people. This group of people, who cannot be certainly identified—though there might be some reference to the affair of Bi'r Ma'ūna (*Medina*, 31–3; *Prophet*, 146–8)—seem to have engaged in hostile activity after making at least a treaty of non-aggression. Muḥammad is now told that unless they make peace, they are to be attacked.

92/4 – 94/6 Believers not to be killed

92/4 if he belong to a people at enmity with you: that is, the victim; this further implies that individuals could become Muslims; note that no blood-wit is given to non-Muslim tribes.

by a compact: this implies a 'people' or rather 'tribe' (*qawm*) in alliance with Muḥammad.

94/6 greeting: Ar. *salām*, that is, the greeting of 'Peace be with you' which was a distinctive Muslim greeting; the believing raider was not to treat such a person as a non-Muslim and so one whom it was permitted to kill and rob.

95/7 – 100/1 Fighting, staying at home, emigrating

95/7 God has preferred ....: those who go out on expeditions and who contribute money and goods are in a superior rank, though it is not clear whether this is in the present life or the life to come. The underlying conception of ranks is also the basis of the Dīwān of 'Umar, according to which the Muslims received graded stipends.

97/9 the angels take: sc. in death; this is said to apply to men who claimed to be Muslims but did not leave Mecca; some are even said to have been killed at Badr.

abased: cf. 75/7; their excuse was that they were persons with no authority and therefore unable to go against the leading men of their clan. The following verse allows that for some persons such a reason may be valid.

emigrate: presumably to some place other than Medina; similarly in 100/1.

101/2 – 104/5 Prayer at moments of danger

101/2 journeying: on a raiding expedition.

102/3 when thou . . . performest . . .: when Muḥammad himself acts as imam or leader.

bow: sc. prostrating themselves; the words might also mean 'when they have bowed (*sc.* and completed the prayer)'.

103/4 a timed prescription: presumably means it is something prescribed for the believers to perform at certain fixed times.

105/6 – 115 Attitude to evil followers

105/6 be not an advocate . . .: the traditional occasion of this passage is that the son of one of Muḥammad's companions stole a coat of mail but denied the theft and managed to get the blame fastened on a Jew; some other Jews gave evidence that the Jew had acquired it lawfully, so making the culprit appear guilty; the brothers of the culprit, however, appealed to Muḥammad to support the son of his companion, and he inclined to do this, until stopped by this revelation. The passage thus emphasizes that the Book (the Qur'ān) is to be the basis of judicial decisions.

108 discourse unpleasing: false evidence (?).

113 a party of them: if the story is correct, these are the kinsmen of the culprit.

116 – 126/5 Idolatory and true religion

116 Cf. 48/51.

117 female beings: the 'daughters of God' as in 53.19 f.; or else angels.

a rebel Satan: this is the Qur'ān's description of what the pagans worship, not their own.

119/8 cut off the cattle's ears: presumably camels are meant; this is a pagan religious practice, cf. 5.102/3.

125/4 took Abraham for a friend: Ar. *khalīl*; cf. *Isaiah*, 41.8; 2 *Chronicles*, 20.7; *James*, 2.23.

127/6 – 130/29 Further rules about women

127/6 a pronouncement: presumably implies that some difficulties were found in applying the previous rules; but these are first reaffirmed.

128/7 prone to avarice: may mean that people cling selfishly to their privileges, or that there was some financial aspect to the agreement.

131/0 – 137/6 Belief and unbelief

135/4 witnesses for God: Muslims are to be just and truthful, in contrast to the old Arab ideal of supporting one's kinsman, right or wrong.

138/7 – 149/8 The fate of the Hypocrites and other opponents

138/7 good tidings: ironically; or perhaps simply 'tidings'.

139/8 unbelievers for their friends: the Hypocrites were in alliance with some of the Jews of Medina (cf. 151/0), perhaps also with pagans.

140/39 when you hear . . .: apparently referring to 6.68/7.

141/0 Did we not gain the mastery . . .: perhaps rather 'were we not superior to you (so that without our help you could not have won)'—this is addressed to the unbelievers.

150/49 – 162/0 Jewish unbelief and wrong-doing

150/49 to make division . . .: explained by the following words. Muslims believe that all prophets and messengers brought the same message in essentials, and that therefore all prophets should be accepted without distinction. In contrast the Jews refused to recognize Muḥammad, and thus could be said to 'disbelieve in part'.

153/2 a Book from heaven: perhaps the Jews demanded something comparable to Moses' stone tables.

154/3 the Mount, etc.: cf. 2.63/0 ff.

156/5 a mighty calumny: an accusation of fornication.

157/6 they did not slay him: basically this is a denial that the crucifixion was a Jewish victory.

a likeness of that: the Arabic phrase is vague and could mean 'a likeness of crucifixion' or 'a likeness of a Jewish victory' or 'a likeness of him, Jesus'. Some of these interpretations are close to Gnostic views.

162/0 the believers believing ...: a few Jews did acknowledge Muḥammad as a prophet.

163/1 – 170/68 Muḥammad is like previous prophets

163/1 Psalms: or 'a scripture'.

171/69 – 173 Criticisms of Christian doctrine

171/69 Three: all the main forms of Christianity would deny worshipping three gods, though popular practice may come near to doing this. Christians worship God, who is one, and yet also in some sense threefold. The criticism is thus primarily of a Christian heresy.

172/0 to be a servant of God: a conception commonly applied to Jesus in the Bible; the Arabic word further suggests humanity, but it is also part of standard Christian doctrine that Jesus is truly man.

174 – 176/5 Miscellaneous

176/5 indirect heirs: Ar. *kalāla*; the precise meaning is not quite clear; cf. v. 12/15.

5
THE TABLE
Al-mā'ida

This sura belongs in the main to the period of the expedition al-Ḥudaybiya and the period after the conquest of Mecca. It has been suggested that some rules about the Pilgrimage are earlier, perhaps soon after Badr.

1 – 5/7 Rules about food and other matters

1 bonds: or contracts or undertakings, and in the latter case the fulfilling of Divine regulations may be included, such as those which follow.

except that which is now recited: except what has been forbidden in the Qur'ān as now recited.

in pilgrim sanctity: that is, while wearing the pilgrim garb or *iḥrām*; this was done for the main ceremonies of the pilgrimage.

2 God's waymarks: Ar. *sha'ā'ir*, perhaps refers to rites and ceremonies, or more generally to cult-symbols.

the holy month: the month or months in which blood-feuds were in abeyance.

the offering: the sheep or other animals to be sacrificed; 'the necklaces' are probably the garlands placed round its neck.

3 move you to commit aggression: this suggests a time not later than the expedition of al-Ḥudaybiya or the pilgrimage (*'umra*) a year later. At an earlier date it was probably possible for

Muslims who were not Meccan Emigrants to join in the pilgrimage; but it was specially the Emigrants who felt 'detestation', or those who had been prevented from going beyond al-Ḥudaybiya. Another possibility is that the aggression envisaged was not connected with a visit to Mecca.

3/4 *excepting that you have sacrificed duly:* that is, the animal wounded by a beast of prey but not killed.

idols: Ar. *nuṣub,* also meaning stones set up, perhaps like the Hebrew *massēba.*

partition by . . . arrows: as in the game of *maysir*; cf. 2.219/6.

3/5 *constrained in emptiness:* constrained in time of famine to eat something forbidden.

5/7 *not in licence:* cf. 4.24/8 f.

6/8 – 11/14 Ablutions, justice, etc

6/8 *for ritual ablutions:* cf. 4.43/6; a variant text gives the sense 'wash your feet to the ankles', and this is Sunnite practice.

8/11 *securers of justice:* cf. 4.135/4.

11/14 various occasions are suggested.

12/15 – 19/22 Criticisms of Jews and Christians

12/15 *twelve chieftains:* the leaders of the tribes who also were the spies sent to Canaan, according to Muslim writers; cf. *Numbers,* 1.4; 13.

17/19 *God is the Messiah, Mary's son:* this is probably not to be taken as a condemnation of all forms of Christian doctrine about the person of Christ, but only of certain heretical forms which would be rejected by the main strands of Christian tradition; the wording is not far from that of doctrines condemned by the Nestorians, especially the doctrine that Mary was Theotokos, 'bearer of God'.

overrule God: the argument seems to be that, since God is omnipotent, the Messiah cannot be thought of as equal in power to him.

18/21 chastise you for your sins: suffering or lack of success is taken as a sign of punishment; a nomadic Arab would not have allowed his son to suffer to the extent to which the Jews and Christians were suffering and failing.

interval: Ar. *fatra*; a long period during which there have been no messengers, usually taken as lasting since the time of Jesus; there is sometimes said to have been a similar interval between Moses and Jesus.

20/3 – 26/9 Israelites refuse to enter Promised Land

23/6 two men: cf. *Numbers*, 14.6.

27/30 – 34/8 The two sons of Adam

27/30 two sons: they are not named in the Qur'ān; for the story see *Genesis*, 4.3–12.

31/4 a raven: the incident is mentioned in Jewish secondary works, though not in the Bible.

35/9 – 43/7 Stealing, unbelief, etc

38/42 the thief: this is one of the few crimes for which a punishment (*ḥadd*) was prescribed in the Qur'ān; the punishment was inflicted, at least until recently, in some more primitive Muslim countries.

41/5 those who say with their mouths: possibly the Hypocrites.

44/8 – 50/5 Judaism, Christianity, Islam

44/8 had surrendered themselves: sc. to God, with the suggestion 'were Muslims'.

49/54 judge between them: this whole passage insists that judgement must be based on revelation.

if they turn their backs . . .: presumably refers generally to the events at Uḥud; cf. 3.155/49.

51/6 – 56/61 Warnings about friendship and apostasy

51/6 friends of each other: this must mean Jews are friends of other Jews and Christians of other Christians.

52/7 those in whose hearts is sickness: the Hypocrites; 'Abd-Allāh ibn-Ubayy was in alliance with Jewish tribes and is said to have tried to stop the expulsion of Banū Qaynuqā' with arguments such as are given here, namely, that the Jews would be useful if Medina were attacked ('a turn of fortune').

55/60 friend: Ar. *walī*, suggesting also 'protector'.

57/62 – 64/9 Jewish mockery and ridicule

60/65 apes: cf. 2.65/1.

worshippers of idols: Ar. Ṭāghūt, perhaps referring to the Calf.

65/70 – 71/5 Other religions

66/70 what was above them . . . beneath their feet: may mean 'what is in heaven and on earth' or, translating 'from what was above them', may mean the rain and the soil.

69/73 Sabaeans: cf. 2.62/59.

72/6 – 77/81 Criticism of Christians

73/7 God is the Third of Three: this is not an attack on the standard Christian doctrine of the Trinity, but on a perversion of it which amounted to the worship of three gods.

75/9 was only a Messenger: though the Qur'ān uses the word *masīḥ*, representing the word 'Messiah' of the Old Testament, there is no exposition of the ideas implied by the word. It should be noted, however, that *rasūl* or 'messenger' comes to mean not simply one who conveys a message but one who executes a commission.

a just woman: who did not claim that her son was divine.

ate food: dependence on the nourishment given by food excludes divinity which presupposes independence; cf. 6.14.

77/81 a people who went astray before: perhaps those who ascribed divinity to Jesus, or the Jews who 'now' refuse to acknowledge Muḥammad.

78/82 – 81/4 The curse on the Jews

79/82 dishonour: disreputable act.

80/3 unbelievers: probably the Meccans with whom some Jews were intriguing both after Badr and before the Siege of Medina: cf. below 'would not have taken them as friends'.

82/5 – 86/8 Christians preferable to Jews

82/5 idolaters: probably the pagans of Medina allied to the Jews.

87/9 – 96/7 Rules about food, oaths, wine, gambling

90/2 arrow-shuffling: Ar. *maysir*; cf. 2.219/6.

93/4 there is no fault . . .: this appears to mean that the eating or drinking of something forbidden is not a serious sin; it is sometimes held that the verse was revealed when some people were anxious about the fate of Muslims who had drunk wine and then died; another interpretation is that it refers to wine-drinking before the revelation that it was forbidden.

95/6 recompense: or compensation.

in flocks: from domesticated animals.

an offering to reach the Kaaba: note the incorporation of old ceremonies into Islam, and the special place given to the Ka'ba.

expiation: this is something of a completely different kind, whereas the 'recompense' seems to be designed to restore to the region of Mecca what had been taken from it.

96/7 game of the sea: fish.

97/8 – 105/4 The Ka'ba; old practices, etc

97/8 God has appointed the Kaaba . . .: the old sanctuary of

Mecca is thus given a place in Islam; this was probably before the change of *qibla*; for the following words cf. v. 2 above.

101 question not: some men are said to have asked whether it was obligatory to perform the pilgrimage every year; Muḥammad was disinclined to give any answer, but eventually said, 'No; but, if I had said "Yes", it would have been'; the conclusion seems to be that men should wait until a revelation comes.

103/2 cattle dedicated to idols: the translator has added these words to explain the Arabic terms which follow. Muslim scholars differed on the precise significance; among the customs mentioned are the slitting of its ears, the forbidding of its use for loads and the restriction of its flesh to males; cf. *EI*², s.v. Baḥīra; J. Wellhausen, *Reste arabischen Heidentums* (Berlin, 1897), 112 f.

104/3 our fathers: this illustrates the deep reverence of the Arabian nomad for the traditional way of life, and the ancestral custom of the tribe.

106/5 – 109/8 Evidence of bequests; ignorance of messengers

109/8 answer: that is, response to his proclamation.

110/9 – 120 The mission of Jesus; the Lord's table

112 a Table: this reflects some half-knowledge of the Christian sacrament of the eucharist that must have reached the Arabs of Medina.

6
CATTLE
Al-an'ām

Muslim scholars regard this sura and the following one as having for the most part been revealed in the year before the Hijra, except for a few verses which were revealed at Medina. This view is generally accepted, but some European scholars would place rather more verses in the Medinan period. The themes are suited to the situation of Muḥammad and the Muslims about the year 621.

1 – 18 God and the unbelievers; God's power

1 the shadows: or darkness.

2 a term: the day of death; the pre-Islamic belief that a man's term was predetermined by some impersonal power is accepted in part by Islam, but the fixing of the 'term' is ascribed to God.

3 earning: by way of reward and punishment for good and bad deeds; so the word almost means 'doing'.

5 that they were mocking: God's punishment, especially in this world.

6 many a generation: the primary reference is probably to the vanished tribes of 'Ād, Thamūd, and others known to the Arabs of the seventh century.

7 a Book on parchment: Muḥammad seems to have been asked to produce miraculously a physical book.

8 an angel: the sending of an angel would have implied that action was imminent, perhaps the end of the world; the next verse says the angel-messenger would have appeared as a man, presumably because only in this way would human senses apprehend him.

12 their souls: or 'themselves'; cf. v. 20.

19 – 32 Authority for the message; unbelievers

19 what you associate: false deities you associate with God by treating as divine.

20 those to whom we have given the Book: presumably Jews and Christians.

recognize it: the Book; 'him' is grammatically possible, and would refer to Muḥammad.

25 some of them: probably the leaders of the Meccans are intended; their outlook was materialistic, and they regarded belief in God as 'fairy tales'.

26 they forbid it: that is, they keep (others) from the Qur'ān.

29 we shall not be raised: they deny resurrection and by implication judgement.

31 the encounter with God: or 'meeting', *sc.* on the Day of Judgement.

33 – 41 Encouragement to Muḥammad in despondency

35 if thou canst seek out ...: the meaning seems to be that, if Muḥammad can find a sign to convince them by penetrating the earth or ascending to heaven (or the sky), he is at liberty to do so, but, even if he finds a sign, it will be fruitless.

36 *answer only will those . . .:* only those who listen to the message with understanding will respond positively.

38 *the Book: sc.* of God's decrees.

42 – 55 The consequences of neglecting God's warnings

42 *nations before thee:* the communities to which the various messengers were sent who are mentioned in the Qur'ān; most were disbelieved.

44 *the gates of everything:* all forms of prosperity.

46 *seizes your hearing . . .:* takes away your understanding of the matter.

sets a seal . . .: makes you unable to respond positively.

47 *openly:* presumably means 'after a warning'.

50 *the Unseen:* perhaps simply the 'future', though elsewhere the word may mean 'the unseen or divine realm'; cf. v. 59.

52 *do not drive away:* this is said to have been revealed when the leading men of Mecca wanted Muḥammad to restrict his dealings with certain poor followers; cf. 18.28/7.

falls upon thee: it is not for Muḥammad to decide whether they are sincere or not.

56 – 73 Muḥammad worships God, who is supreme

58 *what you seek to hasten:* the punishment to fall on the unbelievers; Muḥammad's opponents had probably scoffed at this.

60 recalls you by night: that is, in sleep, though the Arabic word is usually applied to death.

that a stated term may be determined: or completed.

61 recorders: angels to record their deeds; some say they are guardian angels.

63 shadows: darkness, with the connotation of trouble and danger.

68/7 those who plunge into our signs: engage in ridicule of them; cf. 4.140/39; probably Jews are intended.

70/69 those who take their religion for a sport . . .: probably pagan Meccans are intended (cf. 8.34 f.), and if so, this would illustrate the lack of true religious devotion in pre-Islamic Mecca.

74 – 90 Abraham's pure belief; his progeny

79 a man of pure faith: cf. 3.67/0.

80 and He has guided me: or 'though He . . .'.

83 in degrees: sometimes interpreted as degrees of knowledge and wisdom.

86 above all beings: sc. the rest of the world.

87 elected: or 'chose'.

91 – 4 The nature of revelation

91 They measured not . . .: this denial of all revelation sounds like an objection of the Meccans, but the following words about 'putting it into parchments' would be more appropriate of Jews.

you were taught: sc. by revelation, presumably Muḥammad's.

God: sc. sent it down to Moses.

92 *the Mother of Cities:* usually taken as Mecca.

93 *he who forges . . . a lie:* towards the end of Muḥammad's life certain false prophets appeared, who claimed to receive revelations, but who were also leaders of revolt against Medina; the best known was Musaylima (cf. *Medina,* 134 f.). It is unlikely, however, that any such had appeared when this passage was revealed. Perhaps the thought is that, if Muḥammad had 'forged a lie', he would be very wicked. It is also possible that some pagan Meccans claimed to be able to produce something similar to the Qur'ān; cf. the challenges to produce a sura in 11.11/16, etc. The story is also told of how Muḥammad failed to notice additions or mistakes made by one of his secretaries, Ibn-Abī-Sarḥ, who later reverted to paganism.

the angels: sc. of death who take away souls.

94 *what we conferred: sc.* wealth; the speaker of the verse is God.

95 – 111 God's power, and the folly of the unbelievers

95 *splits:* that is, when they sprout.

96 *a reckoning:* days, months and years are based on the movements of the sun and moon.

98 *a lodging-place and a repository:* said to mean the loins of one's father and the womb of one's mother; cf. the pre-existence of Adam's progeny in his loins, 7.172/1 f.

100 *as associates the jinn:* presumably refers to worshippers of idols, who probably did not themselves say they were worship-

ping jinn; this is rather the assertion of others about the worshippers and has been taken up by the Qur'ān.

104 watcher: Ar. *ḥafīẓ*, or 'keeper', referring to Muḥammad; cf. v. 107 and 88.22.

105 thou hast studied: the opponents accuse Muḥammad of having gained information from Jews and Christians.

108 Abuse not . . .: Muḥammad's uncle, Abū-Ṭālib, is said to have been asked, when dying, to persuade him to act in this way.

112 – 22 Opposition to Muḥammad; good laws

112 revealing: or 'suggest', Ar. *yūḥī*, the technical word for 'reveal' but the use here may not be technical.

122 who was dead . . . life: this is said to refer to a convert to Islam, perhaps Ḥamza or 'Umar.

123 – 35/6 Opposition of Meccans or Jews

123 great ones . . .: leaders of the wicked people in it; probably refers to the Meccans.

125 expands his breast: makes it easy for him to surrender to God, that is, become a Muslim.

128 have made much of mankind: that is, have been much concerned with them, seeking to tempt them and lead them astray.

131 unjustly: that is, before they had been warned and had had an opportunity of repenting.

133 from the seed of another people: probably means that the Meccans followed on previous guardians of the Ka'ba with whom they had some ties of blood.

135 according to your station: that is, their position of power and authority (addressed to the Meccans); Muḥammad will not be deflected from his course.

136/7 – 147/8 Pagan rites and taboos: Muslim food laws

136/7 This is for God: the simplest meaning is that God has a share in the offering along with the idols; He might have been regarded as a superior but more remote being.

137/8 to slay their children: to do so was a custom among the pagan Arabs, perhaps in part due to the pressure of population on food resources (v. 151/2); it is condemned in various passages of the Qur'ān.

138/9 f. cattle: cf. 5.103/2.

141/2 pay the due thereof: probably means the *zakāt*, sometimes translated 'legal alms', which was a kind of tithe.

145/6 I do not find in what is revealed to me . . .: this passage summarizes the Islamic regulations about meat, and also explains that further restrictions were placed upon Jews as a punishment.

146/7 with claws: this is the proper meaning of the Arabic word, but it may be intended to represent the 'cloven hoof' of *Leviticus*, 11, and *Deuteronomy*, 14.

148/9 – 153/4 God only to be worshipped; His commands

152/3 in the fairer manner: probably meaning so as to improve it.

when you speak, be just: probably means, when you give a judgement, do so impartially, and do not favour your kinsmen.

154/5 – 158/9 The Book given to Moses and Muḥammad

154/5 complete: usually said to mean 'a complete or perfect rule or code of conduct'.

155/6 This is a Book: the Qur'ān.

156/7 upon two parties: Jews and Christians.

157/8 a clear sign: the Qur'ān so far as revealed; some Meccan objectors excuse their unbelief by saying they have had no opportunity of studying the previous scriptures, or by complaining that they have not a Book like the Jews and Christians; the reply is that they have something similar, but that they fail to respond to it.

159/60 – 165 Muḥammad's religion is distinct

159/60 those who have made divisions . . .: Jews and Christians.

161/2 the creed of Abraham: this is the Qur'ānic claim, made about the time of the break with the Jews, that Muḥammad is recalling men to the pure religion of Abraham (the father of the Arabs as well as of the Israelites)—a religion which has been corrupted by Jews and Christians.

162/3 ritual sacrifice: Ar. *nusuk*, may also mean other forms of ritual worship.

those that surrender: Ar. *muslimīn*, 'Muslims'.

164 bears the load of another: probably not directed against Christian doctrine, but emphasizing that the judgement is on the individual and that kinsmen cannot help.

165 viceroys: as holding God-given dominion in the earth.

7
THE BATTLEMENTS
Al-a'rāf

This sura, like the previous one, is mainly late Meccan, though a few verses may be Medinan.

1 – 9/8 God's judgements

2/1 impediment: or doubt, because of the slight response.

7/6 we shall relate to them: sc. what they have done.

10/9 – 25/4 Adam and Iblīs

20/19 Satan: to be identified with Iblīs. For the story of the temptation; cf. *Genesis*, 3. Iblīs is thought to be derived from the Greek, *diabolos*.

25/4 from there . . . brought forth: raised from tombs in the earth at the resurrection.

26/5 – 34/2 Reflections on the story of Adam, etc

26/5 feathers: anything used primarily for adornment; cf. the English 'fine feathers'.

28/7 indecency: Ar. *faḥisha,* probably some pagan sexual custom forbidden by Islam; the excuse is based on the deep Arab reverence for ancestral tradition.

29/8 set your faces: does not necessarily mean they are to face a particular *qibla*; might simply mean 'direct yourselves to God'.

sincerely: that is, solely.

31/29 your adornment: usually taken to mean 'best clothes': it is probably intended to exclude the nudity of some pagan worship; for nudity or partial nudity cf. 2 *Samuel,* 6.20.

35/3 – 51/49 Judgement on those who reject messages

37/5 they have gone astray . . .: the idolaters are abandoned by the beings (perhaps jinn) whom they worshipped.

40/38 until the camel passes through the eye of the needle: the same phrase is used in *Matthew,* 19.24; *Mark,* 10.25; *Luke,* 18.25. Both Muslim and Christian commentators mention the possibilities that 'camel' means a thick rope, and that 'needle' means a small side-gate.

46/4 veil: or 'partition'; this, which comes between Paradise and Hell, is said to be a wall; cf. 57.13.

on the Ramparts: Ar. *al-a'rāf,* the plural of *'uruf,* 'an elevated place'. The men on the *a'rāf* may be either the prophets or persons who are in an intermediate state between Paradise and Hell.

48/6 the dwellers on the Battlements: the same Arabic word as for Ramparts.

49/7 are these . . .?: the inhabitants of Paradise.

52/0 – 58/6 The Book; God's power and goodness

53/1 *interpretation:* that is, the fulfilment of the promises and threats.

intercessors: the pagan Meccans seem to have thought that their deities would intercede for them. Muslims of later times held that God would allow Muḥammad to intercede for Muslims.

54/2 *the creation and the command:* God creates all animate and inanimate things, but he also gives moral and ritual commands to conscious beings (men, angels, jinn).

59/7 – 64/2 Noah

60/58 *the Council of his people:* the word for 'council' (*mala'*) is that used for the 'senate' at Mecca, and the word translated 'people' (*qawm*) often means a tribe. This illustrates how the descriptions of previous messengers often mirror conditions in Mecca.

63/1 *by the lips of a man:* cf. the Meccans' hope that there would be some clearly supernatural manifestation.

65/3 – 72/0 Hūd, the messenger to 'Ād

69/7 *successors after the people of Noah:* this indication of time is unusual; cf. v. 74/2; also 51.46; 53.52/3.

70/68 *that thou promisest us:* the punishment.

71/69 *names you have named:* the false gods.

73/1 – 79/7 Ṣāliḥ, the messenger to Thamūd

73/1 the she-camel of God: the commentators tell a story of how the people of Thamūd demanded a sign, and agreed that both they and Ṣāliḥ should call on their gods, and that all should accept the one who answered. The idols gave no answer, but, when Ṣāliḥ prayed, a rock travailed and brought forth a camel which immediately gave birth to a foal. Most of Thamūd, however, refused to acknowledge God and eventually killed the she-camel. This miracle of the she-camel's appearance is not mentioned in the Qur'ān.

74/2 hewing its mountains into houses: Thamūd are almost certainly the former inhabitants of al-Ḥijr or Medā'in Ṣāliḥ in north-west Arabia, where rock-hewn tombs are still to be seen.

77/5 they hamstrung the she-camel: the stories say that it frightened the other camels from the pastures.

80/78 – 84/2 Lot

80/78 indecency: Ar. *faḥisha*, here of course referring to sodomy.

85/3 – 93/1 Shu'ayb, the messenger to Midian

85/3 fill up the measure and the balance, and diminish not: this is the chief distinctive feature in the story, but the precise reference is unknown.

86/4 barring from God's way: perhaps reflects conditions in Mecca.

94/2 – 102/0 Conclusion of the 'punishment stories'

102/0 no covenant: that is, they broke or failed to observe the covenant by not obeying God's commands.

103/1 – 137/3 Moses and Pharaoh

114/1 near-stationed: cf. comment on 3.45/0 and 26.42/1.

116/3 a mighty sorcery: presumably what is meant is that their rods became serpents as in *Exodus*, 7.11 f.

127/4 shall slaughter their sons: presumably referring to the command to kill the male babies in *Exodus*, 1.22.

133/0 the flood: the Nile is said to have risen much more than usual because of excessive rain; this does not correspond to any of the plagues mentioned in *Exodus*.

137/3 the land We had blessed: Palestine.

138/4 – 158 Moses and the children of Israel

142/38 thirty nights: the commentators say that Moses had to fast for thirty nights as a preparation for receiving the Law; the additional ten nights were, according to some scholars, those during which God discoursed with Moses. According to *Exodus*, 24.18, Moses spent forty days and forty nights in the mount.

successor: the word also suggests the meaning 'deputy'.

150/49 He said, Son of my mother . . .: Aaron addresses Moses; in the following verse Moses prays.

155/4 seventy men: cf. comment on 2.56/3; also *Exodus*, 24.1,9.

157/6 the Prophet of the common folk: Ar. *an-nabī al-ummī*, perhaps 'gentile prophet'; cf. note on 2.78/3. This is of course Muḥammad; and it is appropriate that Moses should pray for him since, as indicated in the following words, the Muslims had come to believe that he had been foretold in the Jewish and Christian scriptures; cf. *Deuteronomy*, 18.15,18; *John*, 14.16; 15.26; 16.7 (the Paraclete).

honour ... dishonour: honourable and dishonourable conduct respectively, or indeed good and bad acts.

relieving them of their loads: this is, of the burdensome prescriptions of the Mosaic law; cf. 2.286.

158/7 O mankind ...: in this verse which is independent of the previous passage, but connected in thought with the previous verse, the universality of Muḥammad's message is asserted by this address to 'men in general'.

159 – 171/0 The people of Moses

160 twelve tribes: Ar. *asbāṭ*, a special word applied only to the Israelites; the tribal character of the Israelites was not clear to the Arabs.

strike with that staff: cf. 2.60/57.

manna and quails: cf. 2.57/4.

161 f.: cf. 2.58/5 f.

163–6: cf. 2.65/1; 4.47/50.

171/0 shook the mountain: cf. 2.63/0.

172/1 – 174/3 God's covenant with mankind

172/1 took from the Children of Adam ...: the usual story is that in a valley near Mecca (or in India) God stroked Adam's back and took from his loins his whole posterity in the form of small ants; all then accepted God as their Lord.

were heedless of this: did not know that God was our Lord.

175/4 – 186/5 People who reject God's signs

175/4 him to whom We gave Our signs: there is no agreement about the identity of this prophet manqué.

180/79 the Names Most Beautiful: the Beautiful Names, usually said to be ninety-nine, have played a large part in Muslim devotion; the theological discussion of God's attributes is also connected with the Names; cf. 59.24.

187/6 – 8 Knowledge of the Hour

187/6 the knowledge of it . . .: cf. *Mark,* 13.32.

189 – 198/7 The origin of man; idolatry

189 out of one living soul: note that Adam is not named; see also Index, s.v. Adam.

194/3 servants: that is, of God.

199/8 – 206/5 Comfort and advice to Muḥammad

199/8 Take . . .: the verbs here are in the singular.

abundance: Ar. *'afw,* but the precise meaning is uncertain; if translated 'abundance', the meaning is that Muḥammad is to accept the voluntary gifts of the people; another translation is 'use indulgence', perhaps meaning he is to pay no attention to insults.

201/0 remember: sc. God, or recollect themselves.

those who are with thy Lord: the angels.

8

THE SPOILS

Al-anfāl

Much of this sura is connected with the battle of Badr in March 624 (*Prophet*, 119–26), but several parts appear to belong to other times.

1 – 19 Reflections on the battle of Badr

1 the spoils: this verse is said to have been revealed shortly after Badr because of a dispute between the older and younger men, and Muḥammad is said to have received the 'fifth' from the spoils of the Jewish clan of Qaynuqā' in the following month.

5 from thy house: from Medina, which was about a hundred miles from Badr.

a part of the believers were averse: some Muslims remained at Medina including Sa'd ibn-'Ubāda (later leader of the Anṣār), allegedly suffering from snake-bite. Presumably such men feared Meccan reprisals against Medina, as indicated by the following words 'as though . . . being driven into death'.

7 the two parties: the Meccan caravan returning from Syria, and the force which came from Mecca to relieve the caravan.

the one not accoutred: not armed, viz. the caravan, which had only thirty or forty guards, whereas the relief force had originally numbered over 900.

to verify the truth: presumably 'the truth (expressed) by His (previous) words' about the complete overthrow of those who rejected His messengers.

9 a thousand angels: cf. 3.124/0.

11 slumber: Muḥammad is said to have been anxious about the outcome of the battle, until he had a short sleep and awoke full of confidence and trust in God.

water from heaven: rain fell during the night and is said to have hindered the Meccans but not the Muslims.

13 made a breach with: or 'resisted'.

15 turn not your backs: a command to stand firm.

17 when thou threwest . . .: traditionally this is made to refer to a miracle which happened when Muḥammad threw gravel against the enemy and so caused them to flee; but the word 'threwest' (*ramayta*) almost certainly refers to the shooting of arrows (cf. *Medina*, 312 f.). The passage is then an assertion that God is the ultimate agent of the victory of Badr, and that men should not pride themselves on it.

19 victory: or perhaps 'a decision': the words are said to be addressed to the Meccans, who are then told to 'give over', that is, desist from attacking Muḥammad; if they 'return' to the attack, God will again attack them.

20 – 35 Appeals and promises to the believers

22 deaf and dumb: to be taken metaphorically; the precise reference is probably to the Meccan pagans.

24 that which will give you life: perhaps war against the Meccans is meant; cf. 2.179/5.

25 a trial: some otherwise unknown danger threatening the whole community.

26 *few and abased:* while they were still at Mecca.

would snatch you away: the word *takhaṭṭaf* means to carry off goods or people, but perhaps the meaning here is the more general one of plunder.

gave you refuge: at Medina.

confirmed you: probably just means that life was made tolerable for them during their first year or so at Medina.

provided you: gave you for sustenance.

29 *a salvation:* Ar. *furqān*; the victory of Badr was regarded as fulfilling this promise of deliverance.

30 *to confine thee:* probably means 'to stop thee preaching'; the following words 'expel thee' show this must refer to the time when Muḥammad was still at Mecca.

32 *rain down upon us stones:* the Meccans say they expect (if Muḥammad speaks truly) a punishment comparable to that of those who disobeyed other prophets.

34 *barring (people) from the Holy Mosque:* presumably the Emigrants and perhaps some of the Muslims of Medina; but some other Muslims seem to have been able to go; cf. 2.217/4 (barring), but contrast rules about pilgrimage, 5.95/6.

36–44/6 Lessons from the battle of Badr

36 *expend their wealth to bar ...:* presumably refers to the Meccan preparations to avenge their defeat at Badr.

38/9 *if they give over ...:* this is perhaps just a taunt, since the Meccans could not have been expected to surrender so easily; cf. v. 19.

39/40 *fight them ...:* the defeat of Badr so provoked the Meccans that there could now be no peace with them.

persecution: Ar. *fitna,* a word of wide meaning; it could mean the persecution of those of Muḥammad's followers still in Mecca; or it might mean all forms of opposition to the religious movement initiated by Muḥammad.

41/2 fifth: Ar. *khums*; cf. v. 1; this was handed over to Muḥammad who was entitled to use it for the persons mentioned next.

the day of salvation: the day of *al-furqān*; this must be Badr, so it is argued that *furqān* must be thought of as a 'deliverance' comparable to that effected by God for the Israelites when they safely passed over the Red Sea while Pharaoh and his army were drowned.

42/3 cavalcade: the caravan returning from Syria.

would surely have failed the tryst: the nomadic Arabs as far as possible avoided fights that were likely to be bloody because the two sides were equally matched; they preferred surprise with overwhelming force; so it appears that the battle of Badr took place because the two sides unwittingly came so close to one another that they could not withdraw without loss of face. The two following verses suggest that, at the moment of the decision to advance or withdraw, each side thought the other weaker than in fact it was.

45/7 – 54/6 The believers have grounds for confidence

45/7 stand firm: this with the later phrase about obedience suggests this passage was revealed after Uḥud.

47/9 swaggering: this is said to be a description of the Meccan relief force under Abū-Jahl.

48/50 no man shall overcome you: the Meccans were unjustifiably confident of success.

49/51 Their religion has deluded them: the mention of the Hypocrites makes it probable this verse and the following ones were revealed after Uḥud; Muḥammad's opponents may well have said that the Muslims had been deluded into over-confidence by their religion.

50/2 the angels take ...: that is, at death; the 'beating' is usually understood as being part of 'the punishment of the tomb' which happens to all after death.

55/7 – 63/4 Treatment of traitors

56/8 they break their compact: this suggests that the passage refers to one of the Jewish tribes, perhaps Qurayẓa, who intrigued with the enemy during the siege of Medina.

57/9 comest upon them: implying capture; they are to be dealt with in such exemplary fashion as to deter other like-minded persons; this may be said to cover the execution of all the males of Qurayẓa (*Prophet*, 171–4).

58/60 dissolve it: sc. the compact with them.

60/2 strings of horses: troops of cavalry; the Muslims are said to have had two horses at Badr, 10 at another expedition to Badr two years later, 36 against Qurayẓa, and 200 against Khaybar (Ibn-Hishām, 693; *Medina*, 257); it is thus probable that this verse refers to the attack on Qurayẓa.

63/4 Hadst thou expended ...: the unity among the Muslims could not have been created by other than religious motives.

64/5 – 71/2 Instructions to Muḥammad after Badr

65/6 twenty of you ... will overcome two hundred: this reflects the optimism of the Muslims after Badr; the next verse, presumably after Uḥud, is still optimistic but less so—'a hundred of you ... will overcome two hundred'.

67/8 until he make wide slaughter: the traditional interpretation is that, while a religion is small, its adherents should kill all idolaters, and not take them prisoner in order to gain ransoms (as the Muslims did at Badr); the crucial word is obscure, however, meaning literally 'making them thick or languid', and perhaps it connotes slaughter until the enemy is decisively beaten. The same word *athkhana* occurs in 47.4, and this latter sense would fit.

68/9 a prior prescription: according to the traditional interpretation this means they could not be blamed for taking prisoners at Badr, because God had previously made lawful for them the spoils and captives. One wonders if there had not perhaps been at a later date some abuse of the practice of taking prisoners; in that case verses 70/1 f., referring to Badr, might be the prior prescription.

70/1 better than what has been taken: belief in God instead of the ransom you have paid.

72/3 – 75/6 Relations of Emigrants and Helpers

72/3 those who . . . have emigrated: the Emigrants from Mecca to Medina up to the date of revelation.

struggled: given money or personal service in arms for the Muslim cause.

those who have given refuge . . .: the Muslims of Medina, often called 'Helpers' (Anṣār).

friends: Ar. *awliyā'*, implies mutual protection; before Badr there had been a formal 'brothering' of each Emigrant with a Helper (*Medina*, 248 f.), and this implied a right to inherit.

those who . . . have not emigrated: one or two important followers of Muḥammad did not emigrate along with him, and clearly he could do little for them while they remained at Mecca; soon after the Hijra, however, members of nomadic tribes became

Muslims, and the following words suggest that it is these who are primarily intended.

75/6 *those who have believed afterwards and emigrated:* may be either later converts and emigrants from Mecca, of whom there were a number after the siege of Medina, or may be converts from nomadic tribes who came to live in Medina (cf. *Medina*, 242). This is presumably revealed later than v. 72/3.

those related by blood . . .: usually interpreted to mean 'nearer to one another than other believers in matters of inheritance, according to the Book of God'; it then abrogates the mutual inheriting by an Emigrant and a Helper who had been 'brothered'.

9

REPENTANCE

At-tawba

This sura deals with various matters connected with war and fighting from the closing years of Muḥammad's life, beginning with the break with the idolaters (about March 631).

1 – 12 Renunciation of pacts; a proclamation

1 an acquittal: Ar. *barā'a*; this means that the 'covenant' or treaty with the idolaters is to cease to be effective after four months; the idolaters in question are probably both the pagan Meccans, and some nomadic tribes. Traditionally, this was revealed after Abū-Bakr had left Medina leading the pilgrimage of 631.

3 the greater pilgrimage: the *ḥajj* as distinct from the *'umra* or lesser pilgrimage; this proclamation (which extends to v. 28) was to be made at the *ḥajj* of March–April 631.

is quit: of contractual responsibility towards them.

4 the idolaters with whom you made covenant: these were probably nomadic tribes with whom Muḥammad had made alliances in the years immediately after the Hijra.

their term: the end of the period stated in the covenant during which it was to be valid.

5 the sacred months: presumably *Dhū-l-qa'da* (xi), *Dhū-l-ḥijja* (xii) and *Muḥarram* (i).

perform the prayer, pay the alms: the basic requirements from those who wanted to be Muslims.

6 *if any of the idolaters . . .:* that is, the old Arab custom of protecting the weak would be observed to the extent of allowing an idolater to remain 'protected' until he had been instructed in Islam and been summoned to become a Muslim; then, if he refused, he was to continue 'protected' until he was out of immediate range of Muslim attack.

7 *at the Holy Mosque: sc.* when Mecca was captured.

8 *if they get the better of you . . .:* there would henceforward be little chance of peaceful coexistence between Muslims and pagans, though the pagans might profess peaceful intentions.

11 *they are your brothers:* acceptance of Islam transformed a man immediately from an enemy to a brother.

12 *if they break their oaths:* that is, the pagans who still had a compact.

no sacred oaths: that is, the oaths are no longer valid.

13 – 24 Renewal of fighting

13 *a people who broke their oaths:* this almost certainly refers to the renunciation of the treaty of al-Ḥudaybiya.

beginning the first time: probably referring to the attack by allies of the Meccans on Muḥammad's allies of Khuzā'a.

14 *healing:* presumably through victory and vengeance—a sentiment common in pre-Islamic poetry.

15 *will remove the rage: sc.* from the hearts of Muḥammad's believing allies.

16 *struggled:* that is, fought.

17 to inhabit: the word *ya'murū* has several meanings; apart from the translation given, the commonest interpretation of this passage is that it forbids idolaters to perform the *'umra* or lesser pilgrimage; but, if this passage was revealed just before the conquest of Mecca, it cannot mean that, and probably means 'to look after and be the guardian of'.

19 the giving of water: the *siqāya* or ensuring the provision of water for the pilgrims was an ancient duty or privilege of one of the clans of Quraysh. It is said that when al-'Abbās, who seems to have fought as a pagan at Badr and been captured, had to meet criticisms of pagan conduct, he retorted that they had also merits, such as providing water for pilgrims (which he did at that time) and looking after the Ka'ba; this verse was then revealed. The verse is addressed to believers, however, and seems intended to reply to the complaint that at the conquest of Mecca custody of the Ka'ba was left in the hands of a pagan family.

24 If your fathers . . .: this verse warns Muslims not to revert, after the capture of Mecca and renewal of contact with their kin, to former relations with unbelievers.

25 – 28 God's help at Ḥunayn; end of the proclamation

25 the day of Hunain (*Ḥunayn*)*:* the battle with the nomads of Hawāzin and Thaqīf shortly aftert he capture of Mecca (*Prophet,* 207–9).

you turned about retreating: the Muslims and their allies were at first over-confident in their 'multitude' of about 12,000 men, but at one point many began to flee until Muḥammad managed to stop the panic.

26 His Shechina: or assurance; cf. 2.248/9.

legions: of angels.

27 *turns towards . . .:* Muḥammad in fact treated the defeated tribes leniently, so that they became firm supporters.

28 *let them not come near . . .:* this seems earlier than verses 2, 3.

if you fear poverty . . .: through loss of trade and the other income from the pilgrims.

29 – 35 Fighting against Jews and Christians; criticisms

29 *Fight those . . .:* apparently directed against Jews and Christians ('who have been given the Book'); but it is then strange that they are described as not believing in God.

tribute: Ar. *jizya,* normally a 'poll tax' of so much per head.

30 *Ezra:* the basis of this criticism is obscure.

33 *the religion of truth:* Islam.

36 – 49 Sacred months; fighting and excuses for avoiding it

36 *the Book of God:* the number was written or ordained in the Book (not the Qur'ān, but the heavenly original or 'preserved table') on the day of creation. By emphasizing twelve the verse excludes the use of an intercalary month every two or three years to make the lunar months accord with the (solar) seasons.

totally: probably means 'in all the months'.

37 *the month postponed:* Ar. *nasī,* the intercalary month; the objection seems to be that it was based on human decisions made at Mecca. By the dropping of the intercalary month the Islamic calendar ceased to accord with the solar years.

38 Go forth: sc. to fight; the objection to campaigning is assumed to be based on a desire for material comfort.

40 God has helped him already: the reference is to Muḥammad's Hijra or emigration from Mecca. He was accompanied only by Abū-Bakr, and the two sheltered in a cave near Mecca until the pursuit of them was abandoned. For Shechina, see v. 26.

42 the distance: these words suggest that this verse and the following ones refer to the great expedition to Tabūk from October to December, 630 (cf. *Prophet,* 218–21).

43 leave: sc. to stay at home.

44 ask not leave of thee: sc. to be excused from struggling (fighting); similarly in the next verse.

46 tarriers: Ar. *qā'idīn,* 'those sitting still', presumably women, children and the unfit.

47 sedition: Muḥammad had some trouble with disaffected persons during and after the expedition to Tabūk.

48 already before: perhaps referring to the movement of opposition which appeared before the siege of Medina (627), but which was completely checked by the failure of the siege; presumably this failure is God's 'command' or 'decision'.

49 give me leave: sc. to stay at home.

do not tempt me: sc. to desert or rebel by exposing me to the hardships of the expedition.

50 – 64 Miscellaneous matters

50 our dispositions: sc. by staying at home.

51 Naught shall visit us . . .: or 'befall us'; the Muslims' anxiety is relieved by their trust in God and in a form of predestination which is closely akin to pre-Islamic beliefs.

52 *the two rewards:* victory or a martyr's death, leading to Paradise.

53 *expend:* contribute to God's cause; lukewarm supporters are no longer to be tolerated.

56 *they are not of you:* though professing to be Muslims, they do not really support you; presumably these are the persons referred to in v. 64/5 as Hypocrites.

58 *freewill offerings:* Ar. *ṣadaqāt,* presumably voluntary contributions given to Muḥammad to be used for various communal purposes mentioned in verse 60.

60 *those whose hearts are brought together:* or 'reconciled'; usually said to be Meccan and other pagans whose support Muḥammad won by gifts; it seems rather that the gifts were made only after men had shown their readiness to support him (*Medina,* 348–53).

in God's way: 'for the cause' or perhaps 'for fighting'.

61 *He is an ear:* perhaps meaning that he listens to malicious gossip and believes it.

65 – 80/1 Criticism of opponents

65 *the hypocrites:* the persons alluded to here (about the year 630) are not the hypocrites of the years 625 to 627 led by 'Abd-Allāh Ibn-Ubayy (cf. *Medina,* 189–91).

66 *plunging:* engaging in conversation.

70/1 *subverted cities:* probably Sodom and Gomorrah.

73/4 struggle with: that is, fight against; cf. 66.9.

74/5 after having surrendered: after professing Islam.

they purposed . . .: some men are said to have plotted to kill Muḥammad on the return journey from Tabūk.

79/80 who find nothing: sc. to give; such men are derided by the hypocrites.

81/2 – 96/7 Reluctance to go on campaign

81/2 left behind: presumably from the expedition to Tabūk.

83/4 if God returns thee . . .: that is, brings him safely back to Medina.

84/5 pray thou never over any one of them: a prayer was said at the grave in Muslim funerals, often by Muḥammad himself. This passage cannot apply to the earlier Hypocrites since Muḥammad said the prayer over 'Abd-Allāh b. Ubayy (cf. Ibn-Hishām, 927).

90/1 the Bedouins: certain nomads, said to be the tribes of Asad and Ghaṭafān.

91/2 those who find nothing . . .: said to be poor tribes such as Juhayna and Muzayna.

no way: sc. to justify punishment.

97/8 – 106/7 The Bedouin and others

98/9 a fine: a payment imposed by force, which they would cease to make when the force was removed.

100/1 the Outstrippers: Ar. *as-sābiqūn*; those who became Muslims at a very early date; soon after Muḥammad's death it became customary to fix a man's stipend according to the date of his becoming a Muslim, the earlier Muslims receiving a higher stipend.

102/3 other have confessed: those who admitted they had done wrong in not going on the expedition to Tabūk.

106/7 others are deferred: the three mentioned in 118/9.

107/8 – 110/1 The mosque 'of dissension'

107/8 those who have taken a mosque in opposition . . .: some Muslims built a mosque at Qubā', towards the south of the oasis of Medina, just before the expedition to Tabūk, and asked Muḥammad to pray in it, but he excused himself; on his return he got some of his faithful followers to destroy the mosque by night, presumably because the builders intended to use it as a convenient place for hatching plots; one of Muḥammad's old opponents, Abū-'Āmir ar-Rāhib, may have hidden in the mosque.

111/2 – 129/30 The believers' rewards and duties

112/3 serve . . . pray: or, 'worship . . . praise'.

those who journey: perhaps those who practise asceticism like wandering Christian monks.

115/6 as to what . . . godfearing: or perhaps 'what they should fear'.

117/8 God has turned . . .: this is connected with the expedition to Tabūk; perhaps Muḥammad himself felt he had been mistaken in excusing some men from taking part; 'the hour of difficulty' may have been the hardships of the long expedition.

118/9 the three who were left behind: three men who stayed away from the expedition to Tabūk without any real excuse, but who had not intrigued with Muḥammad's opponents, were 'sent to Coventry' for fifty days until this verse was revealed.

120/1 that is because they are smitten ...: that is, whenever they are smitten by thirst, etc. a good deed is written to their account.

tread any tread: perhaps 'make any attack'.

122/3 to go forth totally: the more probable interpretation is that, when tribes accepted Islam, they were not all to go to Medina for instruction, but to send a small group from the tribe; sometimes, however, the words are interpreted *as* going out altogether to fight.

127/8 then they turn away: it is suggested that this is because they are afraid a fresh revelation will bring further proof of their disaffection and sin.

128/9 a Messenger from among yourselves: cf. 3.164/58.

10
JONAH
Yūnus

This sura is perhaps mostly late Meccan, but a few verses are Medinan.

1 – 10/11 God's creative power; belief and unbelief

4 *creation:* or 'a creature'.

5 *stations:* the signs of the zodiac; the Arabs were familiar with the solar year, though the Qur'ān prescribed a lunar year.

11/12 – 21/2 Various criticisms of pagan Meccans

11/12 *would hasten good:* perhaps in their seeking wealth.

12/13 *he calls Us:* in prayer.

15/16 *Bring a Koran other than this:* this is said to be a reply to pagans who wanted some compromise, with less condemnation of their present way of life.

16/17 *a lifetime:* Muḥammad was said to be about forty when the revelations began.

18/19 *intercessors:* this suggests that the local deities were regarded as a kind of spirit who would intercede for men with the supreme God.

19/20 a word that preceded: a decree postponing their punishment for unbelief.

21/2 hardship: said to be a famine at Mecca.

a device: they charged Muḥammad with falsehood.

messengers: recording angels.

22/3 – 24/5 A storm at sea; this life is transient

22/3 run with them: with the people in them.

25/6 – 30/1 The future life: the judgement

30/1 prove: or 'experience'.

1/2 – 36/7 Arguments against polytheism

31/2 provides you: provides sustenance for you.

36/7 surmise: baseless opinion.

37/8 – 45/6 The Qur'ān not produced without God

37/8 a distinguishing: a setting out of the particulars distinctly.

46/7 – 56/7 The threatened punishment

46/7 call thee unto Us: in death before the punishment falls.

47/8 is decided between them: between the Messenger with his followers and those who did not believe.

51/2 you seek to hasten it: by asking the Messenger to bring about a demonstration of the reality of the punishment.

57/8 – 70/1 God's goodness and knowledge: the idolaters' folly

59/60 some of it unlawful: by pagan taboos; cf. 6.138/9.

61/2 any Koran of it: any lection (or recitation) included in the Book.

68/9 a son: Ar. *walad,* which does not emphasize the maleness of the child; what is criticized is probably pagan teaching and not Christian.

71/2 – 74/5 Noah and other Messengers

71/2 your associates: false deities 'associated' with God.

75/6 – 93 Moses and Aaron

83 a seed of his people: said to mean some of the younger Israelites; a few scholars apply 'his' to Pharaoh.

prodigals: or 'extravagant persons'.

94 – 103 Assurance to Muḥammad, etc

94 if thou art in doubt: Muḥammad himself must at times have been in doubt.

98 the people of Jonah: the inhabitants of Nineveh to whom he was sent; all the other peoples mentioned in the Qur'ān were punished for disobedience.

104 – 09 Muḥammad's religion

❦ 11 ❦

HOOD

Ḥūd

Mainly late Meccan with some additions from Medina.

1 – 11/14 The Book; God's knowledge and power

3 to every man of grace: Ar. *faḍl*, which is also 'bounty'; probably means that every man who has merited Paradise by his good works will enter it.

12/15 – 24/6 Encouragement to Muḥammad

12/15 thou art leaving: sc. unpublished or undone.

16/19 their deeds there . . .: their deeds (in this life) will (in the life to come) . . .

20/2 the chastisement shall be doubled: said to mean they will be punished both in this life and the life to come.

21/3 that they forged has gone astray . . .: their belief in idols.

25/7 – 49/51 The story of Noah

29/31 I will not drive away . . .: this reflects Muḥammad's resolve not to abandon poor or humble followers when requested by the rich to do this; cf. 80.2 note.

30/2 *if I drive you away:* read 'drive them away'.

36/8 *None of thy people ...:* probably reflects Muḥammad's realization that he would gain no more followers until he left Mecca.

40/2 *the Oven boiled:* according to Jewish tradition the waters of the flood were boiling.

except for him against whom ...: this is said to have been a son or grandson or step-son or adoptive son of Noah; it was also held that Noah's wife, the boy's mother, perished, in accordance with 66.10.

44/6 *El-Judi:* Ar. al-Jūdī; the name of a mountain in Arabia, which may have been connected with the story of the Flood in pre-Islamic times; later Muslim scholars identified al-Jūdī with the Armenian Ararat, also known as Qardu (of which Jūdī might be a corruption).

46/8 *it is a deed not righteous:* that is, Noah's intercession for an unbeliever (even though a son); to avoid the attribution of sin to a prophet some Muslims adopted the interpretation 'he is (doer of) a deed not righteous'.

50/2 – 60/3 The story of Ad and Hood

52/4 *loose heaven in torrents:* give plentiful rain; Ad are said to have suffered a three years' drought.

52/5 *strength:* said to refer to children, their wives having been barren during the drought.

61/4 – 68/71 The story of Thamood and Salih

62/5 a source of hope: it is said they had wanted to make him prince.

69/72 – 82/4 The story of Abraham and Lot

69/72 Our messengers: the angels who came to Abraham at Mamre; cf. *Genesis*, 18.

70/3 he was suspicious of them: according to Arab ideas to refuse food was a sign of hostility; they refused because as angels they did not require food—probably an idea derived from Jewish sources.

73/6 O people of the House: either the family of Abraham from which all future prophets were to proceed (since Muḥammad and the Arabs were descended from Ishmael); or the Ka'ba at Mecca as the centre of the pure worship of God.

74/7 he was disputing with us: about the punishment of the innocent with the guilty; cf. *Genesis*, 18.23–32.

78/80 they are dearer for you: or 'purer', since to give up the guests would be more dishonourable; cf. *Genesis*, 19.8.

83/4 marked with thy Lord: or in His presence; said to mean either that they had special colourings or markings or that each had on it the name of the person it would kill.

84/5 – 95/8 The story of Midian and Shuaib

86/7 God's remainder: said to mean the eternal reward.

87/9 to do as we will: that is, that we should leave off doing as we will.

91/3 but for thy tribe . . .: the tribe or family, even if disapproving of Shuaib, would have felt bound to avenge him, if he were wounded or killed; this was Arab custom, and Muḥammad benefited from it similarly.

96/9 – 109/11 Moses; comment on the stories

98/100 evil the watering-place: the metaphor is that of a herdsman leading his herd to water; a possible translation of this phrase is 'evil the herd led to water'.

110/12 – 123 Encouragement to Muḥammad

114/6 nigh of the night: or 'the former part of the night'; the rule here is said to reflect Meccan practice and to mention three of the five standard times of prayer: dawn, sunset, supper.

121/2 according to your station: your present condition.

12
JOSEPH
Yūsuf

Of all the longer suras of the Qur'ān this is most nearly a unity. Most of it probably was revealed in the late Meccan period.

1 – 3 Introduction

3 *heedless:* with no knowledge of the story.

4 – 22 Joseph put away by his brothers

4 *I saw eleven stars . . .:* cf. *Genesis*, 37.9.

6 *interpretation of tales:* usually taken to be dreams.

8 *his brother:* that is, his full brother (Benjamin).

9 *that your father's face may be free . . .:* that you may have no rivals for his favours.

10 *pit:* or 'cistern'.

20 *dirhams:* a dirham is a silver coin.

23 – 34 Joseph and the Egyptian's wife

23 *the woman:* no name is given in the Qur'ān, but in later tradition she is Zulaykha.

24 the proof: according to one common account he saw the angel Gabriel.

25 thy folk: in particular, wife.

31 come forth: addressed to Joseph.

35 – 53 Joseph in prison

35 after they had seen . . .: usually interpreted 'although they had seen the signs of his innocence'; it is said either that they considered him guilty despite the proofs or that Zulaykha, hoping to make him compliant, alleged that he must be got away for a time until she had recovered from her passion.

49 will be succoured: or 'will have rain'.

press: sc. grapes or olives for wine and oil.

50 what of the women . . .?: this is usually taken as an indirect request by Joseph to have his innocence established.

52 That, so that he may know . . .: spoken by Joseph, 'so that the Governor may know . . .'.

54 – 69 Joseph's brothers come for corn

59 equipment: provisions and other things they needed.

62 merchandise: what they had bartered for the corn.

63 was denied: has been denied for the future.

our brother: Benjamin.

64 his brother: Joseph.

68 a need in Jacob's soul: a precaution implying lack of trust in God.

70 – 87 Joseph tricks his brothers

75 he shall be its recompense: that is, he will become a slave.

76 according to the king's doom: it is said that, according to the laws of Egypt, a man could not be made a slave for theft; but 'God willed' it, in that the brothers previously agreed to slavery.

77 was a thief before: stories are told alleging thefts, real or pretended, by Joseph.

83 'No!' he said . . .: Joseph is speaking.

86 I know from God . . .: said to mean either that he had supernatural knowledge that Joseph was alive, or that he was convinced Joseph's dream would be fulfilled.

88 – 101/02 Jacob and his family come to Egypt

99/100 his mother: said to be not Rachel but Leah, who had taken the place of Rachel after her death.

101/2 in true submission: or 'as a Muslim'.

102/3 – 111 Encouragement to Muḥammad

107 no enveloping of the chastisement . . .: or 'no overwhelming affliction as a punishment . . .'.

13

THUNDER

Ar-ra'd

This sura is mostly late Meccan, and seems to consist entirely of short passages.

1 – 4 Signs of God's power

2 distinguishes the signs: makes them distinct.

3 two kinds: said to mean sweet and sour, black and white, large and small.

5 – 18 God's power and knowledge

6/7 hasten the evil: bring God's punishment on them quickly, despite the obvious examples of such punishment.

8/9 shrinking and swelling: or by how much the births anticipate or go beyond the due time.

15/16 as do their shadows also: this is said to mean that the long shadows of morning and evening appear to be prostrating themselves.

17/18 that over which they kindle fire: the reference is to metal-working.

19 – 29/8 Believers and unbelievers

19 remember: are reminded (of God by the message), accept the reminder and act upon it.

21 join what God . . .: said to mean believe in all the prophets equally.

26 outspreads and straitens . . .: gives provision abundantly or else diminishes it; so also 17.30/2, etc.

30/29 – 43 Encouragement to Muḥammad, etc

31/0 a Koran: a separate revelation, apparently regarded as a word or formula possessing power; the miracles mentioned are said to have been among those demanded by the Meccans.

32/1 a shattering: an overwhelming calamity.

36 those to whom we have given . . .: presumably Jews and Christians, but the reference must be to their attitudes at an early stage in Muḥammad's preaching.

the parties: probably Jewish and Christian sectaries.

37 an Arabic judgement: a rule of judgement in Arabic.

38 wives and seed: said to be a reply to Jewish criticisms of the number of Muḥammad's wives.

every term has a Book: is written down.

41 diminishing it in its extremities: said to mean that the land of the Meccans was diminished by the conquests of the Muslims; cf. 21.44/5.

43 the unbelievers: perhaps Jews.

14
ABRAHAM
Ibrāhīm

This sura is late Meccan or early Medinan, and consists of short passages.

1 – 4 Introduction

4 with the tongue of his people: this is in line with the insistence that the revelations to Muḥammad constitute an Arabic Qur'ān.

5 – 17/20 Moses and other Messengers

5 the Days of God: His favours to them, or perhaps 'the days when He fought for them', on the analogy of the phrase 'days of the Arabs', meaning their battles.

6 women: presumably female children.

9/10 thrust their hands . . .: obscure, perhaps expressing indignation.

18/21 – 23/8 The unbelievers

18/21 earned: or 'done'.

24/9 – 27/32 The parable of the good and bad trees

24/9 a good word: commentators suggest the profession of God's oneness, or the invitation of men to Islam; similarly the 'corrupt word' (v. 26/31) may be acknowledging many gods or opposing God's prophets.

28/33 – 34/7 Unbelievers; duties of believers; God's gifts

28/33 exchanged the bounty of God . . .: probably means that instead of being grateful for God's goodness to them they were disobedient and unbelieving; this could apply to the Meccans.

35/8 – 41/2 Abraham's prayer for Mecca

35/8 make this land secure: sc. the territory of Mecca where bloodshed was forbidden.

36/9 rebels against me: presumably 'rejects the message I bring of God's oneness'; the idea of the following words may be that God will help him to repent, but one commentator says that at this point Abraham did not realize that God does not pardon idolatry.

37/40 some of my seed: Ishmael and his descendants are said to have settled near Mecca; there is 'no sown land' because of the lava flows.

hearts of men: or 'some mens' hearts', i.e. of the Arabs.

41/2 forgive . . . my parents: this is alleged to have been said before he realized his parents were opposed to God, for prayer for unbelievers is forbidden.

43/4 – 52 God's promise and punishment

44/5 defer us to a near term: let us live a little longer.

48/9 the day the earth shall be changed . . .: some commentators say 'into another earth' (or 'a new earth').

15

EL-HIJR

Al-Ḥijr

Probably late Meccan in the main.

1–15 Relations of unbelievers and prophets

2 *will wish that . . . surrendered:* will at some future date wish they had become Muslims; they are to be left as they are now, since their punishment will come in due time.

6 *possessed:* Ar. *majnūn*, dominated by jinn, who would not necessarily convey truth.

8 *with the truth:* or 'on the right occasion' or 'with judgement'; God does not send angels to comply with the Meccans' request, but to bring revelations or execute His judgements; when they come for the latter purpose, the pagans will have no respite.

14 *Though . . . still they mounted:* either the Meccans or angels.

16–25 Signs of God's power

16 *constellations:* probably the signs of the zodiac.

17 *every accursed Satan:* or 'every stoned demon'; the Satans are said to have tried stealthily to observe the inhabitants of Paradise, and to have been driven away by stones, which

appear to men as shooting stars (hence 'a manifest flame'), cf. 37.6–10.

20 *those you provide not for:* said to be members of one's family and household, who are really provided for by God; or else, wild animals.

24 *who press forward:* perhaps 'die earlier'.

26 – 50 The story of Iblis

27 *of fire flaming:* elsewhere Iblīs alleges that his refusal to worship is because of his superior (fiery) nature.

36 *the day they shall be raised:* the day of resurrection.

51 – 77 The angels visit Abraham and Lot

53 *cunning:* or 'wise'.

63 *that concerning which . . .:* punishment and destruction.

64 *with the truth:* or 'with judgement' (as v. 8).

70 *forbidden thee all beings:* perhaps means 'forbidden thee to have them as guests'.

78 – 99 The Thicket; El-Hijr; encouragement

78 *the dwellers in the thicket:* Ar. *ayka*; perhaps to be identified with Midian since their messenger is Shu'ayb.

79 *the two of them:* either the folk of Lot and the dwellers in the thicket, or the latter and Midian.

80 the dwellers in El-Hijr: identified with Thamūd; cf. the hewing of houses in v. 82 with 7.74/2.

85 pardon thou: Muḥammad is to pardon the injuries done to him by unbelievers.

87 seven of the oft-repeated: Ar. *mathānī*; the reference is obscure and there has been much discussion of the verse and 39.23/4; Richard Bell (*Introduction*, 119–28) argues that it describes the 'punishment stories', of which the seven main ones are: 'Ād, Thamūd, Midian, and the peoples of Noah, Abraham, Lot, Moses.

88 pairs: or 'couples' (Ar. *azwāj*), who would be given sons; the word might mean 'classes' and these would enjoy wealth.

90 the partitioners: probably the Jews and Christians who accepted parts of God's revelation (their own scriptures) and rejected others (the Qur'ān).

16

THE BEE

An-naḥl

Seems to be partly Meccan and partly Medinan.

1 – 21/2 Signs of God's power

1 God's command: perhaps referring to the promised punishment.

2 of His command: or 'with His affair'.

4 a manifest adversary: said to be revealed in connection with a Meccan pagan, Umayya ibn-Khalaf, who brought arguments about the possibility of resurrection.

10 trees: Ar. *shajar*; perhaps 'shrubs', 'bushes'.

12 subjected to you: that is, to service for you.

13 that which He has multiplied . . .: animals and plants.

14 ornaments: such as pearls and coral.

seek of His bounty: by commerce.

15 firm mountains lest it shake: the Muslims are supposed to have thought the earth would move like the planets but for the mountains.

22/3 – 40/2 Replies to objections of unbelievers

27/8 their building: sometimes said to be the tower of Babel.

28/9 you made a breach: or 'in respect of whom you were in opposition (to the Messenger)'.

29/30 whom the angels take: sc. at death.

41/3 – 47/9 Emigration; Messengers and opponents

41/3 those that emigrated: sc. from Mecca to Medina.

44/6 to mankind: or 'to the people' (Ar. *an-nās*).

48/50 – 69/71 God's power and unity; He has no children

53/5 it is unto Him that you groan: this may describe persons who acknowledged God as supreme in moments of great stress, but at other times acknowledged lesser beings as deities.

57/9 their desire: sc. sons; cf. 53.21.

59/61 trample it into the dust: referring to the practice of female infanticide.

62/4 that they themselves dislike: either daughters or 'associate gods'.

64/6 they were at variance: perhaps Jews and Christians.

69/71 a drink of diverse hues: honey.

70/2 – 90/2 God's relations with men

70/2 the vilest state of life: old age.

71/3 that their right hands possess: slaves.

75/7 a similitude: both this and the following similitude are interpreted as contrasting God with idols.

78/80 hearts: the heart was the seat of intelligence for the Arabs.

79/81 subjected: made to serve God.

80/2 houses: tents.

81/3 coverings: things that give shade like trees, houses, mountains.

shirts to protect you from your own violence: coats of mail.

87/9 that they were forging: the false deities.

91/3 – 105/7 Oaths; questions about the Qur'ān

92/4 one nation being more numerous . . .: obscure; perhaps it means, as is sometimes said, that the tribe of Quraysh would break an alliance with one group if it saw that another was stronger.

93/5 one nation: or religious community.

95/7 for a small price: do not abandon belief in God for this-worldly gifts and advantages offered by the pagans.

98/100 when thou recitest . . .: referring to the possibility that

Satan might intrude some unauthentic words into the revelation (cf. 22.52/1).

101/3 when We exchange a verse . . .: this is usually understood by Muslims as referring to cases where the effect of one verse has been abrogated by another verse revealed later; but the application may be wider and include cases where the earlier abrogated verse has been 'forgotten' (cf. 87.6 f.) and omitted from the actual text of the Qur'ān.

103/5 only a mortal: various names, such as those of Christian or Jewish slaves, are given for the person alleged by the Meccans to be helping Muḥammad to produce the Qur'ān; this verse does not deny that Muḥammad had meetings with such a person, but insists that the person in question could not have helped to produce the text of the revelations since he was 'barbarous', a foreigner (Ar. *a'jamī*) and not a native Arabic speaker.

106/8 – 128 Various matters: apostasy; the punishment of unbelief; unlawful food; Abraham; instructions to Muḥammad

106/8 excepting him . . . compelled: it is said that a faithful follower renounced Islam when persecuted by the Meccans, and was later told by Muḥammad that it would not be counted against him.

112/3 a city that was secure: this suggests Mecca in the first place, but the description fits most of the 'punishment stories' (cf. comment on 15.87); it is difficult to be sure whether the 'chastisement' had happened or was still to happen.

118/9 those of Jewry: the Jews' additional restrictions on the use of food are regarded as a punishment; cf. 62.5.

what We related to thee before: cf. 6.146/7.

126/7 if you chastise . . .: sc. by way of retaliation.

17 THE NIGHT JOURNEY

Al-isrā'

Most of this sura is probably late Meccan, but a few verses are certainly Medinan.

1 The Night Journey

1 carried His servant by night . . .: this presumably describes a vivid dream or other mystical experience of Muḥammad, though Muslim scholars have usually regarded it as a physical experience; traditionally, after reaching the Furthest Mosque Muḥammad was carried up into the seven heavens, and there are elaborate descriptions of this 'ascension'.

the Furthest Mosque: (Ar. *al-masjid al-aqṣā*), traditionally identified with the mosque in the temple area at Jerusalem, near the Dome of the Rock. Modern scholars have suggested that this identification was a part of Umayyad propaganda, during the occupation of Mecca by Ibn-az-Zubayr (680–92), to induce Muslims to make a pilgrimage to Jerusalem instead of to Mecca; it is not impossible that 'the furthest Mosque' was originally understood as some shrine nearer Mecca.

2–8 A warning to the Jews

5 the promise of the first: the precise reference is disputed; Goliath and Sennacherib are possibilities.

7 enter the Temple: this might refer to the conquest of Jerusalem by the Romans, if the statement is taken as indicating something which has already happened; but the verbs might also refer to the future, and would then imply something expected in Muḥammad's lifetime.

9 – 21/2 The choice before men

11/12 prays for evil: out of ignorance.

13/14 his bird of omen: signifying the fate decreed for him.

a book: the record of his deeds.

22/3 – 39/41 Duties of believers

28/30 seeking mercy . . .: implies that present circumstances prevent him from helping, but he confidently hopes to be in a position to help in the future.

29/31 keep not thy hand chained: do not be niggardly.

33/5 except by right: the commentators note that the Sharī'a makes death the penalty for apostasy, adultery and murder.

to his next-of-kin authority: that is, to avenge; the infliction of injury and death continued to be punished according to the *lex talionis*, though men were encouraged to accept a blood-wit instead of a life.

let him not exceed: there was a tendency to exact more than a life for a life.

34/6 in the fairest manner: so as to improve it.

shall be questioned of: a man will be held responsible for this.

36/8 that thou hast no knowledge of: perhaps dubious opinions; but the verse is sometimes said to forbid giving false evidence.

40/2 – 60/2 Arguments with unbelievers

41/3 have turned about: have used arguments of various kinds.

42/4 would have sought a way: would have attacked.

46/9 thy Lord only: denying the pagan deities.

52/4 tarried a little: in the grave.

57/9 are themselves seeking: the false deities are regarded as angels.

60/2 when we said to thee . . .: the nearest verse to this is 85.20.

the vision: sometimes taken as referring to the night journey of v. 1; but it may refer to something not mentioned elsewhere.

the tree: perhaps az-Zaqqūm (see Index).

61/3 – 72/4 Iblis; God's goodness

64/6 share with them . . . wealth . . . children: said to mean 'instigate them to seek wealth in evil ways' and to refer to the giving of theophoric names to children such as 'Abd-al-'Uzzā, 'servant of al-'Uzzā'.

73/5 – 81/3 Muḥammad tempted to compromise; worship

73/5 near to seducing thee: probably refers to the affair of the goddesses or 'satanic verses' (cf. 22.52/1 and 53.19,20); it is sometimes said to refer to Muḥammad's inclination to give special terms to the people of aṭ-Ṭā'if (about the year 631), but this is hardly possible in view of the date.

forge . . . another: something other than the Qur'ān.

76/8 near to startling thee from the land: probably refers to some incident at Mecca, but the precise reference is uncertain.

78/80 at the sinking of the sun: the sunset prayer; but sometimes said to mean the midday prayer, when the sun has begun to sink.

the darkening of the night: the last evening prayer.

79/81 keep vigil a part of it: before the Hijra Muḥammad and his followers spent a part, perhaps a large part, of the night in worship; cf. 73.1–6; at Medina their responsibilities made this practice difficult, and it is abrogated by 73.20.

80/2 with a just ingoing . . . outgoing: it is sometimes said this means a satisfactory entrance to Medina and departure from Mecca at the Hijra; but this is probably mere conjecture, as is also the suggestion that it means entering the grave and emerging at the resurrection.

81/3 the truth has come: Muḥammad is said to have repeated these words when he entered the Ka'ba in triumph in January 630.

82/4 – 100/2 The Qur'ān; objections to the Messenger

85/7 the Spirit is of the bidding . . .: or 'is of the affair (*amr*) . . .'; some think the angel Gabriel is meant, and there is probably some connection with revelation; see Index of Proper Names.

93/5 till thou goest up . . .: it has been suggested that the Meccans made this demand because Muḥammad had circulated the story of his night-journey; but it may be that the ascension was added to the night-journey because of this verse.

95/7 walking at peace: presumably implies their being normal inhabitants of the earth.

100/2 for fear of expending: and so exhausting them.

101/3 – 111 Moses; God's power; the Merciful

101/3 nine signs: may be taken as nine miracles, viz. changing the rod into a serpent, making his hand leprous, and seven plagues, variously named; or may refer to nine basic commandments.

104/6 a rabble: perhaps implying 'all together' for judgement.

106/7 at intervals . . . successively: this is a reply to the demand to produce a book miraculously.

107/8 those who were given the knowledge before it: Jews and Christians in their scriptures.

108 Our Lord's promise: perhaps the sending of a prophet.

110 the Merciful: Ar. ar-Raḥmān; the supreme deity had been worshipped under this name in parts of Arabia.

18
THE CAVE
Al-kahf

Mainly Meccan, with one or two Medinan verses.

1 – 8/7 The purpose of the Qur'ān

4/3 a son: or 'child'; probably indicating Arab pagans.

9/8 – 21/0 The Story of the Men of the Cave

9/8 the Men of the Cave: usually identified with the Seven Sleepers of Ephesus of Christian legend; they were young men who hid in a cave to avoid a persecution of Christians under the emperor Decius and fell asleep for many years.

Er-Rakeem: Ar. ar-Raqīm; may be the men's dog or the village nearest to the cave, etc. or some completely separate incident.

21/0 the promise of God: said to be the resurrection, symbolized by the waking of the Seven Sleepers.

21/0 – 31/0 Disputes about the story

21/0 when they were contending . . .: that is, the people of the neighbouring town; the young men were said to have died almost immediately in some versions.

24/3 but only, 'if God will': this phrase of 'reservation' (*istithnā'*) is frequently on the lips of Muslims; cf. *Epistle of James*, 4.13–15, '... you who say, "Today or tomorrow we will off to such a town and spend a year there ..." Yet you have no idea what tomorrow will bring ... What you ought to say is: "If it be the Lord's will, we shall live to do this or that."'

32/1 – 45/3 The similitudes of two men and of water

34/2 in respect of men: this may mean 'family' or less probably 'retinue'; cf. v. 39/7 and 74.13 'sons to dwell before him'. The rich arrogant man presumably represents the pagan merchants of Mecca.

45/3 it is straw: or 'stubble', that is, the broken remains of dried up plants; the subject should perhaps be 'they' referring to 'plants'. The point of the similitude seems to be the mutability of the things of this life.

46/4 – 53/1 The Day of Judgement, etc

47/5 the earth coming forth: perhaps means that it stands forward so that it can be plainly seen.

muster them: sc. mankind.

48/6 as we created you: said to mean 'naked'.

you asserted ...: that is, they supposed He would not fulfil his promise of bringing them to judgement.

49/7 leaves nothing behind: that is, 'omits nothing'.

50/48 to be your friends: or patrons (*sc.* as deities).

54/2 – 59/8 The message and the responses to it

55/3 the wont: Ar. *sunna*; the Arabs believed as a matter of principle in always following the 'beaten track' of previous generations.

58/7 they have a tryst: the threatened encounter with God for judgement, whose time is fixed, though not known to men.

59/8 those cities: the ones described in the 'punishment stories'.

60/59 – 82/1 Moses and 'the Servant'

60/59 when Moses said ...: this is clearly an old legend of the Middle East.

64/3 This is what we were seeking: they are said to have been told that, where they lost the fish, they would find a man wiser than Moses.

65/4 one of Our servants: usually identified with a legendary prophetic figure al-Khidr (also identified with Elias).

83/2 – 98 The story of Dhū-l-Qarnayn

83/2 Dhool Qarnayn: Ar. Dhū-l-Qarnayn, literally, 'Lord of the two horns'; usually identified with Alexander the Great. Those who asked are said to have been Jews. The details of this story are explained in several different ways.

99 – 110 Replies to various objectors

99 surging: probably referring to the tumult on the Day of Judgement.

19

MARY

Maryam

Mostly late Meccan or perhaps early Medinan.

1 – 15 Zachariah and (John the Baptist)

5 I fear my kinsfolk: according to some Muslim commentators the next of kin were his brother's sons who were wicked men and might have led people to idolatry.

a kinsman: or 'successor' (Ar. *walī*).

7/8 No namesake: cf. *Luke,* 1.61, 'there is nobody in your family who has that name'.

12/13 forcefully: literally 'with power'; perhaps, as some suggest, with a resolution to observe it.

13/14 tenderness: or 'grace' (Ar. *ḥanān*).

16 – 33/4 The story of Mary and Jesus

16 mention in the Book: this implies that at the time of the revelation Muḥammad is engaged in producing a Book comparable to those of Jews and Christians; in earlier revelations he had been commanded to proclaim messages to his fellow citizens or to his followers.

17 took a veil: this and various other features of the story come from an apocryphal Christian book, the *Protevangelium Jacobi* (translated by M. R. James in *The Apocryphal New Testament*, Oxford, 1924, etc., 38–49).

Our Spirit: identified with the angel Gabriel.

24 the one that was below her: either the child or Gabriel; other translations are possible.

28/9 Sister of Aaron: European scholars usually explain this as due to confusion with Miriam, the sister of Moses and Aaron. Both Mary and Miriam would be 'Maryam' in Arabic. This conclusion is not absolutely necessary, however, and Muslim scholars have given many possible explanations; e.g. that Mary really had a brother called Aaron, that she was sister of Aaron as being of Levitical stock, etc. Perhaps one might say this was a misconception current among the Arabs which the Qur'ān did not find it necessary to correct; cf. 3.36/1.

34/5 – 40/1 Disputes about Jesus

37/8 the parties: perhaps Jews and Christians.

41/2 – 50/1 Abraham

44/5 the All-Merciful: Ar. ar-Raḥmān; used at various points in this sura as a proper name; cf. 17.110.

51/2 – 63/4 Moses, Ishmael, Idris and their successors

51/2 devoted: or 'single-hearted'.

52/3 in communion: that is, private conversation.

54/5 true to his promise: many Muslims (but not all) hold that it was Ishmael whom Abraham prepared to sacrifice, and interpret this phrase of that incident; but such an interpretation is not necessary.

56/7 Idrīs: sometimes identified with Enoch who 'walked with God; and he was not for God took him' (*Genesis*, 5.24). It has also been suggested that the name is derived from Esdras, the Greek form of Ezra.

58/9 bore with Noah: in the ark.

64/5 f. The function of the angels

64/5 We come not down . . .: these two verses are understood as being spoken by the angels in their own name.

66/7 – 80/3 Objections of Meccan pagans

71/2 he shall go down to it: it is held by many Muslims that even the believers will be brought near to Hell, but the fire will not be able to hurt them.

73/4 which of the two parties . . .: it is implied that the believers are inferior in wealth and social position, but there will be a reversal of fortune in the world to come.

74/5 furnishing: goods, wealth.

80/3 that he says: that is, his wealth and children.

81/4 – 96 Criticisms of polytheism

82/5 they shall deny . . .: that is, the gods.

83/6 to prick them: instigate them to greater sin.

84/7 a number: sc. of days or years.

88/91 a son: probably referring to pagan views; cf. 21.26.

97 f. The purpose of the Qur'ān

98 We destroyed: sc. because they disbelieved such a message as the Qur'ān.

20

TA HA

Ṭā' Hā'

Probably late Meccan in the main.

1 – 8/7 The Qur'ān is from God the omnipotent

2/1 unprosperous: probably implying 'through the poor response to the proclaiming of the message'.

9/8 – 40/2 The story of Moses – his call

15 I almost conceal it: this is best taken as a parenthesis, meaning that knowledge of the Hour is not widespread; the purpose of its coming is that souls may be recompensed.

16/17 bar thee from it: from believing in it.

25/6 open my breast: that is, prepare me to receive spiritual instruction easily.

27/8 the knot: Moses, according to some Jewish stories, had an impediment in his speech.

29/30 familiar: or 'minister' (Ar. *wazīr*, vizier).

39 loaded on thee love from Me: said to mean 'caused those responsible for Moses to love him'.

to be formed: instructed.

41/3 – 82/4 The story of Moses – struggle with Pharaoh

67/9 *sliding:* it is said that the appearance of movement came from the use of quicksilver; elsewhere the ropes and staffs are said to have become serpents.

70/2 *what is in thy right hand:* his staff, which became a serpent and swallowed the other serpents, as described elsewhere, but only implied here.

78/80 *overtaking:* Pharaoh's overtaking you.

81/3 *exceed not:* do not transgress by ingratitude or insolence.

83/5 – 101 The story of Moses – the people's sin

85/7 *the Samaritan:* Ar. Sāmirī, not a proper name, but commentators purport to reproduce the name; for the connection of the worship of the calf with Samaritans, cf. *Hosea,* 8.5.

90/2 *no more:* that is, 'that is all', 'only'.

102 – 112/11 Aspects of the Last Day

103 *you have tarried:* *sc.* in the grave.

106 *a level hollow:* or 'a bare or desert plain'.

113/12 f. No impatience in receiving the Qur'ān

114/13 *hasten not:* do not be overhasty either in repeating the Qur'ān after Gabriel or in publishing it; perhaps Muḥammad was anxious about meeting demands for instruction.

115/4 – 127 Adam's covenant

123/1 each of you an enemy to each: 'you' is here plural, whereas in the previous line it was dual; the plural is to be understood as 'you men and Satan'.

124 blind: as a punishment for misuse of sight.

128 – 35 The need for patience

129 it had been fastened: perhaps means 'the punishment would be close at hand or inevitable'; it must wait until its predetermined time.

132 We ask of thee no provision: the normal interpretation is that God does not require Muḥammad to work to provide for his family; but the words might mean that God did not require offerings as the false deities did.

21
THE PROPHETS
Al-anbiyā'

Mostly late Meccan.

1 – 18 Those warned and the messengers

5 a poet: poets are severely criticized in the Qur'ān (cf. 26.224–6), probably because they were thought to be inspired by jinn, or were associated with the humanistic attitudes of the nomadic tribes.

12 Our might: sc. threatening their city, they ran out of it, *sc.* the city.

19 – 29/30 Angels and false deities

22 they ... to ruin: 'they' is dual, referring to 'earth and heaven', and the thought is that they would be ruined by the conflict of the rival gods.

glory be ... above ...: the thought is that God must be held to be too sublime for the earthly qualities ascribed to him (such as having peers).

24 him who is with me: him (or those) who are contemporary with me.

26 a son: or 'child', probably referring to pagan ideas, cf. 19.88/91.

30/1 – 47/8 God's power; objections to Messengers

30/1 all sewn up: that is, solid or cohering.

31/2 firm mountains: cf. 16.15.

44/5 diminishing it: cf. 13.41.

48/9 – 50/1 Moses and Aaron

48/9 the Salvation: (Ar. *furqān*); see note on 2.53/0.

51/2 – 73 Abraham

51/2 rectitude: usually taken as 'direction', and regarded as given through books of revelation.

74 – 7 Lot; Noah

78 – 82 David and Solomon

79 We made Solomon to understand it: according to Islamic tradition David decreed that the sheep which had strayed and eaten a crop of corn should be forfeited to the owner of the corn; but Solomon argued that the latter should have only the produce of the sheep until the field was restored (i.e. milk, lambs, wool).

we subjected . . .: the mountains and the birds were to promise God.

80 *garments:* coats of mail.

81 *the wind:* is said to have carried his throne.

83 – 90 Job; Ishmael, etc.; Jonah; Zachariah

87 *Dhul Nun:* 'him of the fish', i.e. Jonah.

90 *set his wife right:* made her capable of conceiving a child, with a suggestion of making her righteous.

91 – 4 Mary

93 *split up their affair:* divide into separate religious communities, such as Jews and Christians.

95 – 100 The Gate of cities destroyed

96 *Gog and Magog:* evil spirits; cf. 18.94/3 ff.

they slide down: 'they' may refer either to Gog and Magog (with their followers) or to the resurrected inhabitants of the cities destroyed ('they' in the previous verse).

97 *the true promise:* the judgement.

101 – 6 The reward of the righteous

101 has gone forth: this is taken to mean 'has been decreed', since it could not be held they already enjoyed Paradise.

far from it: from Hell; it is said by some Muslim scholars that this passage was revealed to make clear that men who had been worshipped as gods (e.g. Jesus and Ezra), would not, if they themselves were upright, be included in the condemnation of v. 98, but would be in Paradise.

105 in the Psalms: cf. *Psalm* 37.29.

107 – 12 The vocation of Muḥammad

107 a mercy: as bringing a message which, if they follow it, will lead to eternal bliss. According to the commentary of al-Jalālayn the translation should be 'in mercy to the worlds' or 'showing mercy to the worlds'.

111 I know not: sc. with regard to the delay of punishment.

112 He said: that is, Muḥammad; a variant reading is 'Say'.

22

THE PILGRIMAGE

Al-ḥajj

Mostly early Medinan, but a few verses in the second half may be Meccan.

1 – 13 The Last Day and the raising of the dead

5 a blood clot: the early condition of the embryo in the womb, just as 'a lump of flesh' describes its later condition.

the vilest state of life: old age.

6 brings the dead to life: the argument for God's power to raise the dead is firstly His power to give life to man in the first place, and secondly His power to revive vegetation.

11 the very edge: means in effect that they 'sat on the fence'; it is said to refer to nomads who professed Islam at Medina.

14 – 24 The contrast between believers and unbelievers

15 stretch up a rope: the verse is obscure; it is sometimes interpreted of hanging oneself, but this is not likely.

25 – 33/4 The Ka'ba and the Pilgrimage

25 the Holy Mosque: the Ka'ba.

who cleaves to it: lives close to it, as distinct from the nomads ('tent-dwellers').

26/7 the place of the House: it is said in Muslim tradition to have been the site of a previous place of worship which was destroyed at the Flood.

that shall go about it: circumambulate the Ka'ba—a primitive part of the ceremonies (also in v. 29/30); the following words refer to other ritual actions.

27/8 the Pilgrimage: this pre-Islamic complex of rites was incorporated with some changes into Islam, and made a duty to be performed at least once in his life-time by each Muslim, if he has sufficient wealth. This verse is usually dated early in the Medinan period, when Muḥammad himself cannot have been in a position to go to Mecca.

28/9 on days well known: animals are sacrificed on a certain day of the pilgrimage.

29/30 finish with their self-neglect: put an end to the state of ritual taboo (*iḥrām*) adopted for the central part of the pilgrimage; the pilgrims now shave their hair, cut their nails, etc.

vows: good works they have undertaken to do during the pilgrimage.

30/1 venerates the sacred things: perhaps refers to respect for the sanctity of the region round Mecca and of certain months; but it might be more general.

32/3 waymarks: cf. 2.158/3 and comment; the word is also interpreted of choice victims for sacrifice, since the following verse probably means that animals for sacrifice may be enjoyed for a time; cf. v. 36/7 below.

34/5 – 37/8 The sacrifice of animals

34/5 may mention God's name: the orthodox Jews still have a similar rite by which meat is rendered 'kosher'.

36/7 standing in ranks: or 'in order'; it is said to mean standing on three feet with the fourth tied up.

37/8 the flesh of them . . .: this is a denial of a primitive Semitic idea (found in the Old Testament) that God was made favourable to men by the physical qualities of the sacrifice, e.g. its smell.

38/9 – 51/0 Fighting against unbelievers; their punishment

39/40 to those who fight: with this reading (*sc. yuqātilūna*) the passage is held to have been revealed shortly before the Hijra and to have been the first permission to the Muslims to defend themselves by force; many Muslim scholars, however, prefer the reading *yuqātalūna*, 'are fought against', which implies that hostilities have started; and the words 'expelled from their habitations' must be after the Hijra.

40/1 some by the means of others: this appears to imply that force is necessary for maintaining the structure of society, including the practice of religion.

46/5 blind are the hearts: the heart is the seat of understanding and intelligence.

47/6 is as a thousand years: cf. *2 Peter*, 3.8, 'one day is with the Lord as a thousand years'; cf. also *Psalm*, 90.4.

52/1 – 54/3 Satan and the revelation

52/1 Satan cast into his fancy: or 'desire'; this passage is a justification for some previous alteration in the text of the Qur'ān; one strand of tradition holds that it applies to verses originally proclaimed as following 53.19,20 (see comment there), but later removed on the ground that they had been falsely inserted by Satan; the verses permitted intercession to pagan deities, and were said to have come to Muḥammad as he was earnestly desiring to find some way of making his religion acceptable to the rich merchants of Mecca. A difficulty, perhaps not insuperable, is that the 'satanic verses' must have been abrogated long before the Hijra, whereas the term 'those in whose hearts is sickness' (v. 53/2) is associated with the period between the battles of Badr and Uḥud.

confirms His signs: here almost certainly 'verses'.

55/4 – 62/1 The Judgement; the Emigrants provided for

60/59 chastises after the manner that he was chastised: that is, avenges an injury but only to the extent of the injury; the words 'then again is oppressed' imply that the original aggressor does not accept the justice of the vengeance.

63/2 – 66/5 God's power

66/5 ungrateful: Ar. *kafūr*, which suggests *kāfir*, 'unbeliever'.

67/6 – 78 Differences in religion; the fate of unbelievers and believers

67/6 every nation: or religious community; the difficulty was presumably due to the fact that some Muslim practices differed from those of the Jews.

73/2 if a fly should rob them: the Jews apparently held that heathen temples swarmed with flies on the sacrificial animals.

78 witness against mankind: perhaps referring specially to Jews and Christians who had not maintained their religion in its purity.

23
THE BELIEVERS
Al-mu'minīn

Traditionally the last sura to be revealed at Mecca.

1 – 11 The Believers

This passage summarizes the duties of believers.

12 – 22 God's creative power

12 an extraction: or perhaps 'fine part', but the thought is obscure.

13 a receptacle: the womb; the following verse—'clot', 'tissue', etc.—describes stages in the growth of the embryo.

14 another creature: that is, a new creature.

17 seven ways: perhaps the paths of the planets are immediately intended, but the ultimate reference is to the seven heavens.

20 a tree: the olive.

21 what is in their bellies: milk.

23 – 30/1 Noah disbelieved

24 *who deserves to gain superiority:* this suggests that Muḥammad's opponents may have been afraid of his gaining political power.

25 *bedevilled:* possessed by one of the jinn. (Ar. *bi-hi jinna*).

wait on him: observe him to see what happens to him.

27 *the Oven:* cf. comment on 11.40/2; also for the person excepted.

31/2 – 41/3 An unnamed community

31/2 *another generation:* usually said to be 'Ād or Thamūd.

38/40 *has forged against God a lie:* this seems to imply that the people of the community had some belief in God, perhaps as a supreme deity.

42/4 – 56/8 Other messengers; Moses; Jesus

51/3 *eat of the good things:* perhaps an implied criticism of Jewish food restrictions.

52/4 *one community:* probably emphasizing the divisions between Jews and Christians.

57/9 – 77/9 God's dealings with believers and unbelievers

61/3 *outracing:* that is, they arrive first.

62/4 save to its capacity: that is, God does not impose any duty on men which they are not able to perform.

63/5 their hearts are in perplexity . . .: this obscure verse probably means that the hearts of certain unbelievers are in such a state that they fail to do the good acts just mentioned, and instead 'have deeds' other than those, and they will continue doing such deeds until punishment comes.

71/3 read 'had surely been corrupted'.

72/4 tribute: though the word usually means a tax, it is often understood here as referring to a reward or payment for the messenger's work of warning, and this seems to fit the context better.

75/7 the affliction: this is said to refer to a famine which afflicted the Meccans.

78/80 – 92/4 God's power and oneness

79/81 scattered: as a sower scatters seed.

85/7 they will say 'God's': cf. also verses 87/9, 89/91; this seems to imply (as v. 38/40) that the people addressed believed in a supreme deity.

88/90 protecting and Himself unprotected: Ar. *yujīr wa-lā yujār 'alay-hi*; that is, in His strength He can guarantee protection to others but no one is strong enough to guarantee protection against Him. The granting of 'neighbourly protection' (*jiwār*) was a normal practice of strong nomadic tribes.

91/3 son: or 'child', presumably against pagans.

93/5 – 98/100 Muḥammad's trust in God

93/5 that they are promised: the punishment.

99/101 – 118 Death and Judgement

100/2 barrier: Ar. *barzakh,* here something which cannot be passed, but in later Islamic thought it became a kind of purgatory for the period between death and resurrection.

113/5 a day: that is, compared with eternity; cf. 22.47/6.

24

LIGHT

An-nūr

This sura deals with 'the affair of the lie' concerning 'Ā'isha, and other matters of about the same date. Muḥammad had taken 'Ā'isha with him on an expedition in January 627 (or a year later according to some authorities). At the last halt on the way home 'Ā'isha got left behind, while looking for a necklace she had dropped at her toilet, and was not missed. Eventually she came back to Medina riding the camel of a handsome young man, who had walked alongside. Gossip seized hold of this incident and malicious allegations of misconduct on 'Ā'isha's part were spread both by a few of her personal enemies, and by Muḥammad's political opponents. She withdrew to her parents' house, until at length Muḥammad received a revelation (probably vv. 10 ff.) declaring 'Ā'isha's innocence. At a public assembly which he called it became clear that his political opponents (the Hypocrites) had now little support in Medina.

1 – 9 The punishment of fornication; the need of evidence

1 *appointed:* perhaps meaning 'made obligatory'.

2 *scourge each one . . .:* this is the only punishment prescribed in the Qur'ān as we have it; some Muslim traditions speak of a 'verse of stoning' (i.e. prescribing stoning, as is done in the Old Testament) as having been included in the Qur'ān; but this is probably a later invention to minimize the difference between the Qur'ān and the Old Testament on this point (cf. *Islam and*

Integration, 192). The verse 4.15/19 is usually said to be abrogated by the present verse, and in any case probably refers to the continuance of pre-Islamic mores. Arabic uses the word *zinā'* for both fornication and adultery, and this verse is usually understood of fornication only because later Islamic law theoretically prescribed stoning for adultery (while making it virtually impossible ever to obtain sufficient evidence).

4 *cast it up:* make imputations of unchastity.

7 *the curse of God:* the calling down of a curse on oneself if one was speaking falsely was thought by the Arabs to have considerable value as evidence; cf. comment on 3.61/54.

10 – 20 The slander against 'Ā'isha

11 *the slander:* Ar. *ifk*, also translated 'lie'.

a band of you: Muḥammad's political opponents led by 'Abd-Allāh ibn-Ubayy.

good for you: presumably meaning that the final outcome of the incident would be good for those chiefly concerned; in particular the weakness of Muḥammad's opponents was made clear.

whosoever of them . . . the greater part: probably means 'the man who was chiefly responsible', namely, 'Abd-Allāh ibn-Ubayy.

12 *the believing men and women:* those who helped to circulate the slander; they were persons who were jealous of 'Ā'isha for various reasons.

13 *four witnesses against it:* the slanderers should have brought four witnesses of the misconduct they alleged.

14 *your mutterings:* literally, 'what you spread broadcast'.

21 – 33 Various prescriptions resulting from the 'lie' and similar matters

21 *indecency and dishonour:* probably meaning sexual irregularity (acceptable in pre-Islamic times) and 'what is not done'.

pure: perhaps meaning 'free from guilt' or 'upright'.

22 *swear off giving:* it is said that at first Abū-Bakr decided to discontinue an allowance he paid to a relative because the latter had helped to spread the slander about 'Ā'isha; but after this verse was revealed he relented.

23 *cast it up:* cast imputations of unchastity.

women in wedlock: Ar. *muḥsanāt,* presumably meaning those who observed the Islamic norm by which a woman had relations with only one man at a time (and then kept an *'idda* or 'waiting period'); cf. 4.24/8.

26 *these are declared quit . . .:* good men and women are declared free of the criticisms made of them by bad men and women.

29 *houses uninhabited:* said to refer to inns, shops, etc.

31 *fathers . . .:* these appear to be men whom they are forbidden to marry.

what their right hands own: slaves.

such men . . . not having sexual desire: old men and the like; it is disputed whether eunuchs are included.

nor let them stamp their feet: sometimes said to mean they were not to make a tinkling noise with their anklets; cf. *Isaiah,* 3.16,18.

33 *contract with them . . .:* the writing of manumission was a declaration by the owner that he would set the slave free on receiving a certain sum of money.

desire to live in chastity: desire to live in *taḥaṣṣun*, presumably meaning that each restricted herself to one man at a time, corresponding to *muḥṣanāt* in v. 23.

34 – 46/5 God's power

35 *God is the Light . . .:* this is known as the 'light verse' (*āyat an-nūr*), and has been given various mystical interpretations; it may describe the lights at the altar in a Christian church.

39 *finds God:* he cannot escape the punishment due for his unbelief; or perhaps 'finds God causing him to die'.

40 *shadows:* or 'darknesses'; the idea seems to be that the works of the unbelievers are unseen because of the darkness, or perhaps are those of people who cannot see where they are going.

43 *send down . . . mountains: sc.* of clouds.

47/6 – 54/3 Attitudes to Muḥammad; obedience

47/6 *a party of them turn away:* presumably referring to the Hypocrites.

48/7 *that he may judge between them:* according to the 'Constitution of Medina' disputes were to be referred to Muḥammad, but it was only gradually that this precept was observed; the commentators name specific persons who quarrelled.

50/49 *sickness in their hearts:* a phrase used to describe the Hypocrites prior to Uḥud.

53/2 *do not swear:* this is said to mean that actual obedience is enough, and false oaths do not help.

55/4 – 57/6 The believers reassured

55/4 *successors:* that is, in power; it almost means 'rulers'"

58/7 – 64 Rules about asking permission

58/7 *ask leave of you: sc.* to enter; the point seems to be that the persons named were to ask permission to enter at the times mentioned in case they should inadvertently see the householder naked, which is forbidden to Muslims; at other times familiar members of the household did not require to ask permission.

63 *the calling of the Messenger:* this might mean they were not to address Muḥammad as they did other men, but to give him a title like 'O Messenger of God'; but it could also mean that more attention was to be paid to Muḥammad's calling *to* them.

25
SALVATION
Al-furqān

Probably late Meccan, with a few verses revealed at Medina.

1 – 10/11 God's purpose for Muḥammad; objections to him

1 the Salvation: Ar. *furqān*; cf. the comment on 2.53/0; in the present verse, however, it is usually said that the Salvation is the Qur'ān (presumably as guiding to salvation), and this fits the context.

2 a son: lit., 'child', referring to pagan views.

4/5 a calumny: or 'fraud'; for the 'other folk' cf. comment on 16.103/5.

8/9 a man bewitched: 'subjected to magic' or 'enchanted'.

11/12 – 19/21 The unbelievers and their punishment

13/14 for destruction: they wish for death to escape from torment.

20/2 – 34/6 Messengers and the Qur'ān

20/2 some of you . . . for others: thus some people through their wealth may be a cause of envy for poor people; the point of the trial is to see whether people will endure (be patient).

22/4 *a ban forbidden:* this is said to be an expression used by Arabs when suddenly and unfairly attacked; it is uttered by the sinners, probably at death, when they see the angels coming to take them away.

24/6 *resting-place:* presumably during the heat of the day.

30/2 *a thing to be shunned:* or perhaps 'a thing uttered deliriously'.

32/4 *may strengthen thy heart:* Muḥammad certainly gained assurance from the fact that he received revelations at frequent intervals.

35/7 – 44/6 Unbelievers destroyed, or threatened

38/40 *Er-Rass:* the word *rass* may mean 'well', but the people have not been identified.

40/2 *rained on . . .:* perhaps Sodom.

45/7 – 62/3 God's power in nature

45/7 *has stretched out the shadow:* the reference is to the long shadows at sunrise; the following words 'made it still' probably mean 'made it the same length'.

the sun to be a guide to it: as the day proceeds the sun becomes an indication of the length of the shadow, and the shadow of the sun.

46/8 *drawing it gently:* causing it gradually to get shorter.

48/50 before this mercy: the winds announce the coming of rain.

52/4 thereby: perhaps meaning 'with the Qur'ān'.

53/5 the two seas: cf. comment on 35.12/13.

54/6 made him kindred: made him increase into a body of people akin by descent or marriage.

60/1 bow . . . the All-Merciful: this is a statement of part of the problem to which 17.110 is the answer; people felt that the All-Merciful (ar-Raḥmān) was a separate god, different from God (Allāh) whom they worshipped at the Ka'ba in Mecca.

63/4 – 77 The qualities of believers

73 fall not down: the sense is obscure, but it is probably contrasted with standing and attending to God's message.

77 My Lord esteems you not: the meaning and reference of this verse is not clear.

26
THE POETS
Ash-shu'arā'

Mainly late Meccan, with a few verses revealed at Medina.

1 – 9/8 The obstinacy of the unbelievers

3/2 consumest thyself: that is, with worry.

4/3 their necks will stay humbled: that is, they will be completely convinced, and unable not to respond.

7/6 of every generous kind: sc. of every kind of good and useful fruit and plant.

10/9 – 51 The story of Moses and Pharaoh

14/13 a sin against me: or 'crime', viz. the killing of an Egyptian; cf. 28.15/14 and *Exodus*, 2.12.

18/17 He said: presumably Pharaoh.

21/0 judgment: that is, jurisdiction.

22/1 a blessing ...: the meaning of this verse is uncertain; another possibility is, 'what I now ask of you is a blessing (or favour) by which you may place me under obligation to you, seeing you have enslaved ...'.

42/1 the near-stationed: in positions of special privilege in the royal court; the word *muqarrabīn* is also used of angels in God's 'court', and is indirectly connected with Hebrew 'cherubim'; cf. comment on 3.45/0.

50 There is no harm: sc. for us in such a death; the words are perhaps rather like our colloquial phrase 'no matter'.

52 – 68 The exodus from Egypt

57 expelled them: that is, caused them to leave.

59 bequeathed them on . . .: caused the Children of Israel to inherit them, either by returning to Egypt or by gaining something equivalent in Palestine.

69 – 104 The story of Abraham

76 the elders: literally 'former', 'previous'; perhaps it simply means 'forefathers'.

84 a tongue of truthfulness: that is, a good reputation (being well spoken of).

105 – 22 The story of Noah

109 my wage falls only upon . . .: it is incumbent on Him only to reward me.

112 what knowledge have I . . .?': this is said to mean 'I (Noah) do not know whether my followers believed for good motives or bad'.

123 – 40 The story of 'Ād and the prophet Hūd

128 a sign, sporting: the 'signs' are said to have been land-marks to indicate the route; they did this 'in sport', since it was not absolutely necessary.

129 haply to dwell forever: this seems to imply 'hoping you will make yourselves immortal'.

137 this is nothing but . . .: sc. this conduct of ours; the phrase may also be taken as a parenthesis so that it means 'this attitude of theirs . . .'.

141 – 59 The story of Thamūd and the prophet Ṣāliḥ

152 set not things aright: that is, are not concerned for good order in the community.

160 – 75 The story of Lot

171 an old woman: sc. his wife, cf. 27.57/8 and 66.10.

176 – 91 The men of the Thicket and Shu'ayb

176 the men of the thicket: to be identified with Midian.

187 lumps from heaven: that is, pieces of the heaven.

192 – 220 The revelation to Muḥammad is authentic, not demon-inspired

193 the Faithful Spirit: eventually identified with Gabriel.

198 a barbarian: that is, not an Arabic-speaker.

214 warn thy clan . . .: this is said to be the beginning of Muḥammad's public preaching.

215 lower thy wing: either 'take under thy protection' or 'deal gently with'.

221 – 27/8 Imposters and poets

223 they give ear: in hopes of hearing some piece of genuine revelation.

224 the poets: the poets were traditionally supposed to be inspired by jinn, and perhaps for this reason are here attacked, especially since they played an important part in forming public opinion (like journalists today); Muḥammad was not wholly hostile to poets, but had one or two who composed poems in his praise and defence.

225 wander: implying they are partly mad.

27
THE ANT
An-naml

Probably late Meccan in the main, but some verses seem to be Medinan.

1 – 6 Believers and unbelievers

3 who perform the prayer . . .: these phrases usually come after the establishment of the Muslims at Medina.

7 – 14 The call of Moses

14 they denied them . . .: they publicly denied the signs because they were wrong-doers and proud men, although they themselves were convinced by them.

15 – 45 Solomon and the queen of Sheba

17 jinn, men and birds: a view found in Jewish tradition, as is also the following idea of 'the Valley of Ants'.

21 or he bring me . . .: that is, 'unless he brings me —'

22 he tarried . . .: sc. the hoopoe.

24 apart from God: or 'and not to God'.

29 *she said . . .: sc.* the queen of Sheba.

31 *in surrender:* presumably meaning 'as Muslims'.

35 *will send them: sc.* Solomon and his people.

36 *when he came . . .: sc.* her envoy.

rejoice in your gift: and in your ability to offer such a splendid gift.

38 *in surrender:* or 'as Muslims'.

39 *efreet:* Ar. *'ifrīt;* one of a specially wicked class of jinn.

40 *he who possessed knowledge of the Book:* sometimes said to be Solomon's vizier, but this is doubtful.

when he saw it . . .: sc. Solomon.

42 *f. And we were given the knowledge . . . in surrender:* apparently spoken by the courtiers in her train, who claim to have been Muslims.

45 *surrender:* connoting 'become a Muslim'.

45/6 – 53/4 Ṣāliḥ and Thamūd

45/6 *two parties:* presumably believers and unbelievers.

46/7 *to hasten evil: sc.* the punishment of unbelief.

47/8 *your augury is with God:* that is, the evil you augur is in God's keeping and is His responsibility, not mine.

49/50 *protector:* Ar. *walī, sc.* the next-of-kin who had the duty of blood-revenge.

54/5 – 58/9 Lot

56/7 that keep themselves clean: or 'that hold themselves to be clean'.

59/60 – 66/8 God's power, uniqueness, knowledge

61/2 a partition between the two seas: cf. 25.53/5, and comment on 35.12/13.

62/3 the constrained: sc. the person in need.

successors: probably implying 'of previous generations'.

63/4 shadows: or 'darknesses'.

bearing good tidings . . . mercy: cf. 25.48/50.

64/5 brings it back again: restores it after death.

provides you: gives you your sustenance.

67/9 – 75/7 Reply to objections about resurrection and judgement

67/9 be brought forth: sc. from the graves to life.

70/2 do not sorrow for them: sc. and their obstinacy.

for what they devise: because of their plots.

76/8 – 79/81 Disputes among the Children of Israel

76/8 they are at variance: probably referring to disputes between Jews and Christians.

80/2 – 93/5 Muḥammad's mission; the Judgement

82/4 a beast: this has become a regular preliminary to the Last Judgement in Islamic tradition; cf. *Revelation,* 13.

85/7 the Word: the sentence of condemnation.

90/2 are you recompensed . . .?: they are punished only for their deeds on earth.

91/3 this territory: the sacred area round Mecca.

28

THE STORY

Al-qaṣaṣ

Mostly late Meccan.

1 – 14/13 The story of Moses; his birth and childhood

7/6 into the sea: Ar. *yamm,* perhaps used here of a large river; cf. *baḥr* in 35.12/13.

8/7 picked him out: took him from the water and into their house, though he was destined to be an enemy . . .

12/11 had forbidden: perhaps only meaning 'had kept him from them'.

15/14 – 35 Moses as a young man

15/14 This is of Satan's doing: some commentators say that Moses struck without intending to kill.

23 until the shepherds drive off: sc. their herds.

32 press to thee thy arm: perhaps almost equivalent to 'pull yourself together'.

35 shall not reach you . . .: they shall not be a match for you two (through magic) because you two have Our signs.

36 – 46 Moses and Pharaoh; comments on the story

38 a fire upon the clay: sc. to bake bricks to build a tower which will reach up to heaven; the underlying idea is similar to that connected with the tower of Babel in *Genesis,* 11.4.

41 appointed them leaders, calling ...: probably means 'made these men leaders or exemplars of unbelief who call (their followers or all men) to the Fire.

46 a people to whom no warner came before thee: this implies that Muḥammad's Meccan contemporaries (or all the Arabs) were different from the people at Mecca in Abraham's time.

47 – 59 Following the Messenger and not following

51 the Word: probably meaning the revelation.

57 They say: sc. the people of Mecca.

snatched from our land: this is a little obscure, since it is difficult to see how the Meccans could all have been driven from their town; perhaps the idea was that they would be exposed to raids because the sacredness of the region would not be observed (cf. 29.67); the reply seems to mean that, if God has looked after them well while they were pagans, He is not likely to do less for them after they worship Him.

60 – 75 The future life; judgement; God's power

63 the word is realised: obscure; perhaps means fulfilment of the threat to fill Hell with men and jinn (cf. 7.18/17; 11.118/20); or perhaps means 'the sentence of condemnation has been passed'.

75 that they were forging: their false belief in pagan deities will disappear and be reduced to nothing.

76 – 82 The story of Korah

76 Korah: Ar. Qārūn; cf. *Numbers,* 16; his great riches are mentioned in extra-Biblical Jewish sources.

78 the sinners shall not be questioned: the point of this is not clear; perhaps it is because God already knows their sins in detail.

83 – 88 Heaven; reassurance to Muḥammad

85 a place of homing: some say this means the future life, where he will be vindicated against the Meccans; some say this was foretelling his return to Mecca, and that the passage was revealed during his Hijra to Medina.

88 His Face: meaning roughly 'Himself'.

29

THE SPIDER

Al-'ankabūt

Partly late Meccan, partly Medinan.

1 – 11/10 Trials of the believers

8/7 if they strive with thee . . .: if this passage was revealed about the time of the battle of Uḥud (625) or later—as is suggested by the word 'hypocrites'—the reference might be to parents still in Mecca.

12/11 f. Reply to unbelievers

13/12 other loads: perhaps the responsibility for leading others astray.

14/13 – 44/3 Stories of previous messengers

14/13 a thousand years all but fifty: so in *Genesis*, 9.29; the Flood took place when Noah was six hundred years old.

19/18 originates . . . then brings it back: the reference is to the death and revival of vegetation; so also below in the words 'causes to second growth to grow'; but this is also a sign of resurrection.

29/8 cut the way: some scholars said it referred to highway robbery; but more probably it referred to some sexual malpractice.

45/4 – 55 Muḥammad's religion; replies to objectors

45/4 is greater: or 'more important' or 'very important'.

46/5 dispute not . . .: this is addressed to all the Muslims, and is doubtless to counteract the bad effect of arguments with the Jews of Medina; the date of this is presumably a few months after the Hijra.

we believe . . .: the Muslim attitude, according to this verse, is acceptance of the previous revelations to Jews and Christians, as all coming from God.

to Him we have surrendered: have become 'surrenderers', that is, Muslims.

47/6 those to whom we have given the Book: the Jews of Medina; but this must have been revealed before they began to oppose Muḥammad, perhaps before the Hijra.

some of these: probably the Meccans.

48/7 recite . . . inscribe: 'recite' here may mean 'read'; Muḥammad was not a reader or writer of books.

56 – 69 Emigration and other matters

56 My earth is wide: this is an invitation to leave places where the worship of God is difficult; it might have been revealed shortly before the Hijra (as v. 47/6 may have been).

61,63 they will say, 'God': these words appear to imply that the persons addressed admitted the existence of a supreme deity whom they called 'God'.

65 *making the religion sincerely His:* this probably implies regarding God as the sole object of worship at this moment of crisis, then later reverting to the other cults.

67 *snatched away:* or 'raided, plundered' (cf. 28.57).

69 *struggle:* Ar. *jāhadū*; the word used later came to connote 'the holy war', but here the sense may be more general.

30
THE GREEKS
Ar-Rūm

Mostly late Meccan, with some Medinan verses.

1 – 5/4 The Greeks

2/1 The Greeks have been vanquished: Ar. *Rūm,* indicating the people of the Eastern Roman or Byzantine empire; the reference is presumably to the loss of Jerusalem to the Persians in 614 or more generally to the Persian advance in the years just before and after that. A variant reading reverses the passive here and the active in the following verse—'have vanquished (been victorious) . . . shall be the vanquished (not victors)'; but the dating of this would be difficult, and it looks as if it was intended to transform the passage into a prophesy of the defeat of the Byzantines by the Muslims (cf. Nöldeke-Schwally, i. 149).

shall be victors: the Byzantine recovery under Heraclius may be said to have begun in 627, though he had some successes in Asia Minor from 622 to 625.

6/5 – 19/18 Aspects of Judgement and Resurrection

11/10 originates . . . brings it back again: the primary reference is perhaps to resurrection here, but the words can also apply to the revival of vegetation.

13/12 associates: that is, pagan deities, because associated with God.

17/16 glory be to God: four of the five times of prayer (or the worship) are mentioned here.

20/19 – 28/7 Signs of God's power

20/19 mortals all scattered abroad: usually taken to mean 'human beings who (by natural increase) have spread widely'.

21/0 might repose in them: or 'might live with them'; for the creation of woman cf. 7.189.

25/4 out of the earth: from the graves, presumably.

28/7 among that your right hands own: your slaves; the point is that they are not treated as equals of their masters in material things; cf. 16.71/3.

29/8 – 45/4 True religion and various objections

30/29 God's original: Ar. *fiṭra*, 'natural disposition'; it is assumed that the religion of Islam is in full accordance with this.

32/1 rejoicing in what is theirs: in the scriptures they have; the reference may be to Jews and Christians.

35/4 such as speaks of . . .: that is, explicitly mentions their false deities and authorizes worship.

37/6 outspreads and straitens: see comment on 13.26.

41/0 for that men's own hands . . .: sc. as a punishment for the sins men have committed.

46/5 – 60 Signs of God's power, and inevitability of some unbelief

51/0 if we loose a wind . . .: sc. a hot dry wind which makes the vegetation wither and become yellow.

55 so they were perverted: or perhaps 'so perverted were they (even in their worldly life)'.

31

LOKMAN

Luqmān

Meccan with some Medinan verses.

1 – 11/10 The Book guides some, but others go astray

6/5 some men there are . . .: or perhaps rather 'one man there is . . .', since it is said to refer to an-Naḍr ibn-al-Ḥārith, a Meccan who could repeat many Persian stories.

take it in mockery: either the way of God or the Qur'ān.

12/11 – 19/18 Lokman's wise advice to his son

12/11 Lokman: a wise man of Arabian legend, mentioned in pre-Islamic poets.

18/17 turn not thy cheek away: seems to mean 'do not be disdainful'.

20/19 – 34 God's power and knowledge

27/6 and the sea —: sc. though the sea was ink (cf. 18.109), to write down the words of God.

32
PROSTRATION
As-sajda

Probably Meccan, except verses 16 to 20.

1 – 9/8 The Book; God's power

10/9 – 14 A problem about resurrection

14 you forgot the encounter of this your day: that is, you forgot you would have to experience this day of encounter with God and of judgement.

15 – 22 Believers and unbelievers

17 no soul knows what comfort . . .: cf. 1 *Corinthians,* 2.9 (quoting *Isaiah,* 64.4), 'eye hath not seen, nor ear heard, neither have entered into the heart of man the things which God hath prepared for them that love him'; this verse of the New Testament was familiar to Muslims and was much quoted.

19 in hospitality for . . .: that is, as a lodging in reward for what they were doing.

21 the nearer chastisement: that is, in this world.

23 – 30 The Book of Moses and the vindication of believers

23 the encounter with him: presumably 'with God'.

28 this Victory: Ar. *fat'ḥ,* literally 'opening'; here it perhaps means 'decision'; that is, God's vindication of the Muslims against their opponents and the punishment of the latter; cf. 8.19 where it is said to have come with the success at Badr.

33
THE CONFEDERATES
Al-Aḥzāb

This sura is entirely from Medina. It takes its name from the siege of Medina in April 627 (xi. 5) by the Meccans and various 'confederates' (*Medina,* 35–9). There are also passages concerning Muḥammad's marriage with Zaynab bint-Jaḥsh about the same time, and other matters concerning his wives (*Medina,* 329–31, 284–8).

1 – 8 The reckoning of kinship and other matters

4 Be as my mother's back: this was a pre-Islamic formula for ending a marriage; but it was not a divorce, since the woman continued to live where she was, but could not marry anyone else; since this was an objectionable state of affairs, Islamic law required either that the words should be retracted and expiation made or that there should be a proper divorce; cf. 58.1.

your adopted sons: that is, those regarded as your sons according to pre-Islamic ideas; this relationship was probably different from that brought about by modern forms of adoption and may often have been automatic; thus Zayd ibn-Ḥāritha, who had been captured as a boy and sold as a slave to Khadīja, became Khadīja's son when she set him free, and then, when Muḥammad married Khadīja, Muḥammad's son, Zayd ibn-Muḥammad. Because of this artificial relationship Muḥammad's proposed marriage with Zaynab bint-Jaḥsh, Zayd's divorced wife, was thought to be incestuous; and this verse asserts that it is not so.

6 *than their selves:* that is, than they are to one another.

his wives are their mothers: in a sense this simply confers an honourable title on Muḥammad's wives, but whether because of this verse or solely because of verse 53, it was accepted that, after Muḥammad's death, no other Muslim might marry his wives; this perpetual widowhood may have been involved in the choice offered to them in vv. 28 f.

nearer . . . than the believers and the emigrants: by 'believers' are presumably meant those of Medina; the verse is taken as cancelling the arrangement by which each Emigrant was given as 'brother' a Muslim of Medina; the word 'friends' (*awliyā'*) in the following clause implies some degree of mutual protection, and may refer to the 'brothers'.

9 – 27 The siege of Medina

9 *a wind:* the event which led to the breakup of the 'confederates' after a fortnight's fruitless siege was a night of wind and storm.

hosts you saw not: angels.

11 *shaken most mightily:* probably meaning in respect of their trust in God.

12 *when the Hypocrites . . .:* this was presumably before Muḥammad's 'show-down' with them over the 'affair of the lie'.

13 *Yathrib:* Medina.

no abiding: that is, at the Trench which was the essential defence of Medina; they wanted to return to the centre of the oasis to defend their 'houses' or forts, in which they felt safe.

14 *entrance . . . from those quarters:* presumably from the south, which was furthest from the Trench; had an enemy force

penetrated the oasis from the south many of the inhabitants would have gone over to them with little hesitation.

19 who swoons of death: sc. through fear of death, or at the point of death.

24 chastise the hypocrites . . . or turn again unto them: in fact Muḥammad was reconciled to ʻAbd-Allāh ibn-Ubayy and his followers.

25 sent back . . . unbelievers: sc. the Meccans.

26 supported them from their fortresses: the Jewish tribe of Qurayẓa in the south-east of the oasis intrigued with the enemy during the siege, and afterwards were besieged in their forts by the Muslims until they surrendered, when the men were put to death and the women and children sold as slaves.

27 a land you never trod: probably means that the Muslims had not been in this district of Medina because of the hostility of Qurayẓa.

28 – 34 The prophet's wives

28 the present life: life in this world, perhaps including the right to marry after Muḥammad's death; cf. v. 6; also comment on 66.5.

set you free: there is no record of any of Muḥammad's wives taking advantage of this 'choice'; but there are lists of women who are said to have been considered as wives for Muḥammad, and some of these may have turned from him at this point.

30 shall be doubled: because of her position of privilege.

32 abject in your speech: or 'wheedling'; presumably when speaking to strange men.

in whose heart is sickness: the phrase was often used of Muḥammad's political opponents; but some commentators here take it of sexual indulgence.

33 *the pagans:* Ar. *al-jāhiliyya al-ūlā*, literally 'the former (time of) ignorance'.

abomination: *sc.* of the pagan ways.

35 f. Men and women of Paradise; obedience to Muḥammad

35 *who have surrendered:* or 'are Muslims'.

37 – 40 Muḥammad's marriage with Zaynab

37 *him whom God had blessed:* Zayd ibn-Ḥāritha.

what God should reveal: Muḥammad's love for Zaynab or thought of marrying her.

had accomplished what he would: *sc.* had divorced her.

We gave her in marriage to thee: presumably by the revelation in verse 4, since the present passage appears to be subsequent to the marriage.

40 *is not the father . . .:* *sc.* although Zayd has been called his son.

41 – 48/7 Encouragement to Muḥammad and the believers

41 *and His angels:* that is, the angels join in blessing.

49/8 – 52 Divorce; Muḥammad's marriage-privileges

49/8 no period: sc. no *'idda* or waiting-period of three months such as was required before remarriage from women whose marriages had been consummated.

50/49 their wages: presumably their dowry or bride-wealth; the phrase is usually taken to mean the wives Muḥammad already had; at his death he had nine wives and one concubine.

what thy right hand owns: slave concubines.

the daughters of thy uncles . . .: members of the family for whom he had a responsibility.

any woman believer . . .: lists are given of women who had been married to him without the marriage being consummated or whose marriage had only been spoken of (cf. *Medina*, 397–9), but there is much obscurity about these lists; probably most Arab tribes wanted to claim a marriage-connection with Muḥammad.

for thee exclusively: that is, it (perhaps the last point about 'any woman believer . . .') is a special privilege for thee.

52 thereafter: usually taken to mean 'after this revelation', but stories are told of arrangements for marriages up to the time of Muḥammad's death.

53 – 59 Respect to be shown to Muḥammad and his wives

53 the houses: each wife had her own house or 'apartment'.

without watching for its hour: sc. without waiting until the meal is ready.

55 touching their fathers . . .: sc. in receiving visits from their fathers.

56 do you also bless him . . .: this is the basis of the pious phrase used after mentioning Muḥammad, *ṣallā 'llāh 'alay-hi wa-sallam,* 'God bless him and give him peace'.

59 draw their veils close: perhaps means 'over their faces'; some of the stories about this verse imply that they did this so as to be recognized and not molested.

60 – 73 Punishment for hypocrites and unbelievers

69 those who hurt Moses: the precise reference is uncertain.

72 We offered the trust . . .: reference also uncertain.

34

SHEBA

Sabā'

Mainly Meccan.

1 – 9 God's praise; He punishes unbelief

2 what comes down from heaven, and what . . .: the commentators mention, as coming down, angels, revelation, rain, and, as going up, angels, men's words and smoke.

10 – 14/13 David and Solomon

14/13 naught indicated to them . . .: the story is told that Solomon before his temple was completed, realized he was about to die and prayed to God that his death might be concealed from the jinn until their building of the temple was complete; then he died as he stood praying leaning on his staff, and his body remained standing for a year until a worm gnawed away the staff; by this time the temple was completed.

15/14 – 21/0 Sheba's fate

16/15 the Flood of Arim: or 'the flood of the dam'; this refers to the breaking of the dam of Ma'rib, which symbolizes the break-down of the irrigation system of the Yemen; inscriptions have been found recording the restoration of the dam about the middle of the fifth century and again at the middle of the sixth; the final break-down is thought to have been in the quarter-century before Muḥammad's birth.

17/16 for their unbelief: or 'for their ingratitude'; similarly 'unbeliever' may be 'ungrateful'.

18/17 the cities that we have blessed: those of Syria and Palestine.

19/18 prolong the stages . . .: they said this either in pride or so that they could claim a higher sum for the hire of camels; the whole story is comparable to other 'punishment stories' in the Qur'ān.

22/1 – 30/29 Various matters

22/1 an ant: usually 'atom'.

no partnership in either of them: sc. heaven or earth; the following 'in them' refers to the deities.

26/5 make deliverance: Ar. *yaftaḥ*; perhaps 'decide'.

28/7 to mankind entire: Muḥammad's mission is here asserted to be universal.

31/0 – 39/8 Judgement on the powerful and rich

31/0 those that were abased . . . that waxed proud: Ar. *ustuḍ'ifū, istakbarū,* literally 'reckoned weak', 'reckoning themselves great', and probably referring to the great merchants (who were also clan chiefs) and to those obliged to accept the decisions of powerful clan chiefs; the latter have evidently allowed themselves to be intimidated, perhaps in the matter of joining in the Hijra to Medina.

36/5 outspreads . . . straitens: (also in v. 39/8); cf. comment on 13.26.

40/39 – Various matters

45/4 they reached not a tenth . . .: probably means that the contemporary unbelievers have not a tenth of the wealth of the previous ones.

46/5 stand unto God: or 'before God'.

your comrade: Muḥammad.

35

THE ANGELS

Al-Malā'ika

Mainly late Meccan, but in view of the mention of 'expending', or giving money and goods for the cause, in verse 29/6, some of the second half may be early Medinan. The title of the sura is sometimes 'The Originator' (*Fāṭir*) from the word in verse 1.

1 – 17/18 God's power and goodness

2 opens: bestows, makes available; 'loose' (below) is similar in meaning.

9/10 a dead land: that is, where all the vegetation is dead after the dry summer months.

11/12 in a Book: sc. the Book in which is written down all that God has predetermined for men.

12/13 the two seas: probably refers generally to the body of fresh water and the body of salt water; the word *baḥr* is applied to large rivers as well as to the sea (as perhaps *yamm* is in 28.7/6). Cf. 25.53/5; 27.61/2; 55.19.

ornaments: e.g. pearls, coral.

14/15 your partnership: that is (probably), your making them partners with God.

18/19 – 28/6 Muḥammad's message and different responses

18/19 no soul laden . . .: this verse emphasizes the individualistic character of judgement; a man cannot be helped or supported even by 'a near kinsman'.

24/2 there has passed away in it: that is, there has been sent to it in the past.

29/6 – 45 Believers and unbelievers and their recompense

39/7 viceroys: Ar. *khalā'if* (pl. of *khalīfa*); Adam was appointed God's viceroy or deputy on earth (2.30/28); but the word may also mean 'successors', *sc.* of previous generations.

40/38 a Book: sc. of revelations, which gives them 'a clear sign' on which to base their belief in God.

43/1 the wont of the ancients: sc. the wont or way (Ar. *sunna*) in which God treated them.

36

YA SIN

Yā'-Sīn

Middle Meccan period, but a few verses may be somewhat later.

1 – 12/11 Muḥammad is divinely commissioned despite the unbelievers

3/2 Envoys: Ar. *mursalīn,* 'those sent'; probably to be taken as identical with *rusul,* 'messengers'.

7/6 the Word: the sentence of damnation, or the predestining word.

12/11 what they have left behind: the traces or memorials they have left on earth.

13/12 – 32 Parable of the unbelieving citizens

13/12 the city: said by commentators to be Antioch when visited by disciples of Jesus.

19/18 your augury is with you: that is, will come true of yourselves.

30/29 those servants: sc. of God, that is, men.

33 – 44 Signs of God's power and goodness

33 that we quickened: by sending rain.

36 of themselves: of human beings.

39 stations: the twenty-eight constellations through one of which the moon passes on each day of the month.

41 their seed: the reference may be to the Ark, but in that case one would expect 'Noah's seed'.

45 – 68 Unbelievers and believers and their future lot

47 Expend of that ...: contributing to feed other Muslims suggests the Medinan period.

51 sliding down: or 'hastening'.

65 hand ... feet: that is, the hands and feet of unbelievers tell of the sins they have committed by their hands and feet.

68 We bend him over ...: that is, make him weak instead of strong; the Arabs regarded this as a miserable condition.

69 f. Muḥammad not a poet

69 It is only ...: that is, the revealed message.

70 the Word: sc. of punishment.

71 – 83 God's power

71 cattle: includes camels; it is chiefly camels that are thought of in the reference to riding and beverages in the following verses; nomads live mainly on the milk of camels, and eat their meat only occasionally; cf. 40.79.

76 their saying: what the unbelievers say.

77 a manifest adversary: that is, openly disputes and rejects the message.

78 his creation: his humble status as a creature, and his inability to make assertions about God from his creaturely knowledge.

37
THE RANGERS
Aṣ-ṣāffāt

Mostly from the middle Meccan period.

1 – 10 God is one and creator; the demons

1 rangers: probably angels standing in ranks.

2 scarers: perhaps angels keeping men from disobedience.

5 the Easts: Ar. *al-mashāriq*; the plural probably indicates the different points at which the sun rises according to the season of the year.

7 to preserve against every rebel Satan: shooting stars ('a piercing flame') were held to be stones flung to drive off demons and prevent them listening to those in Paradise; cf. 15.17.

8 the High Council: sc. of the angels.

10 a fragment: of conversation, or of wisdom.

11 – 39/8 Objections of the unbelievers and their fate

11 ask them: sc. the unbelievers.

28 These say: sc. men, addressing the demons who had led them astray.

40/39 – 61/59 The believers in Paradise

52/0 a confirmer: one who accepts the truth of the revealed message.

62/0 – 74/2 Hell and unbelievers

62/0 The Tree of Ez-Zakkoum: the name is also applied to a tree which grows in the region between Mecca and the coast and which is thorny and has very bitter fruit.

75/3 – 82/0 Noah

75/3 the Answerers: sc. 'how excellent are We at answering'.

83/1 – 100/98 Abraham rejects the idols

86/4 a calumny: or falsehood.

89/7 I am sick: the point of this is not clear.

101/99 – 113 Abraham ready to sacrifice his son

101/99 a prudent boy: usually said to be Ishmael.

102 steadfast: patiently enduring.

103 surrendered: sc. to God's will.

upon his brow: Abraham had flung his son face downwards.

107 a mighty sacrifice: sometimes said to imply 'fat' and to be a ram; but the point has been expanded in various ways by later Muslims.

114 – 22 Moses and Aaron

117 the Manifesting Book: that makes clear or is clear.

123 – 32 Elias (Elijah)

125 call on Baal: cf. 1 *Kings*, 18.17–21.

133 – 48 Lot; Jonah

141 was rebutted: that is, the lot fell against him.

145 upon the wilderness: sc. upon the bare shore.

and he was sick: circumstantial; *sc.* being already sick from the time in the whale.

149 – 66 God has no children

150 the angels female: the 'daughters of God' (pagan deities) were sometimes regarded as angels.

164 of us: sc. of the angels.

167 – 82 The unbelievers to be left alone

170 they disbelieved in it: or 'have disbelieved in (the Qur'ān)'.

38

SAD

Ṣād

Meccan, about the middle period. Traditionally the first part (up to v. 15/14) was revealed shortly after the conversion of 'Umar when some of the leading Meccans went to Muḥammad's uncle Abū-Ṭālib to get him to restrain his nephew.

1 – 15/14 The opposition of the Meccan leaders

1 Sad: the name of an Arabic letter, the velarized S.

7/6 in the last religion: perhaps means 'in any religion hitherto'; or, less probably, 'in the religion of our forefathers'.

10/9 ascend the cords: ascend into heaven by cords (ropes) or by 'ways of access'; cf. 40.36/8.

11/10 host of parties: perhaps means 'army of heathen peoples'.

12/11 he of the tent-pegs: this is said to mean that he tied people to four tent-pegs and then tortured them; but this explanation is uncertain.

16/15 – 29/8 David; the settlement of a dispute

16/15 hasten . . . our share: sc. of worldly goods; perhaps spoken in mockery.

19/18 to him reverting: sc. to join in praising God; or returning to God in penitence.

22/1 two disputants: said to be two angels; cf. Nathan's parable in 2 *Samuel*, 12.

24/3 intermixers: those who administer common property.

30/29 – 40/39 Solomon

31/0 the standing steeds: Solomon was said to have a thousand horses which he had captured in war against Damascus and other places; one day he had them paraded for inspection, but became lost in admiration for them and omitted his prayer at sunset; then in penitence for this omission he sacrificed all except a hundred.

33/2 to stroke their shanks and necks: sc. in admiration, before he realized he had forgotten the prayer; less likely is the interpretation 'stroke with the sword', implying the beginning of the sacrifice.

34/3 a mere body: there is a story (from Jewish sources) to explain this reference; to punish Solomon for negligence in allowing a wife to worship an idol, a demon was one day able to get possession of Solomon's signet while he was at his toilet; the demon then gave himself the appearance of Solomon and occupied the throne for forty days, while Solomon received the appearance of a beggar and had to live by begging.

41/0 – 48 Job and others

42/1 this is a laving-place: the implication is that when Job stamps, this cool place for washing appears.

44/3 strike therewith: for some fault of his wife's Job had sworn to give her a hundred strokes if he recovered.

49 – 64 Paradise and Hell

59 this is a troop: usually said to be spoken to those who led the unbelievers astray; but it might be said by these leaders to one another; the unbelievers reply in the next verse.

60 forwarded it: sc. deeds which brought us to this.

65 – 70 Muḥammad and the message

69 the High Council: sc. angels.

71 – 85 Iblis

85 I shall assuredly fill Gehenna . . .: elsewhere (11.118/20; 32.13) God swears to fill Gehenna with jinn and men together; since Iblīs is here called an angel (v. 73 f.), it would seem that jinn and angels may be identified.

39
THE COMPANIES
Az-zumar

Probably about the end of the Meccan period.

1 – 7/10 God's oneness and power

2 making thy religion His sincerely: worshipping God alone to the exclusion of all others.

3/4 in nearness to God: this seems to express the view of non-Muslims that local deities were intermediaries between their worshippers and the supreme God.

6/8 eight couples: usually taken as 'eight (in four) couples', referring to sheep, goats, camels, oxen; cf. 6.143/4 f.

creation after creation: that is, in several stages; cf. 22.5.

in threefold shadows: or 'darkness'; said to be of the belly, the womb and the membranes enclosing the foetus.

turned about: sc. from God to idols.

8/11 – 20/1 Obedience to God and its reward

11/14 of those that surrender: of the Muslims.

21/2 – 26/7 God's power and justice

23/4 consimilar: literally 'resembling itself'; perhaps 'self-consistent'.

its oft-repeated: cf. comment on 15.87.

27/8 – 37/8 Similitudes; God's justice

30/1 in whom partners disagreeing share: the worshipper of idols is compared with a slave jointly owned by several men.

31/2 you shall dispute: Muḥammad will show that he duly conveyed the message to them, and they will repeat their excuses for not believing.

38/9 – 41/2 Trust in God

38/9 that you call upon . . .: the pagan deities, even if angels. have no power against God.

39/40 I am acting: sc. as I think right.

42/3 – 48/9 God brings death, appoints intercessors, judges

42/3 He withholds that . . .: all souls go to God in sleep, but come back to normal life until it is their appointed time ('stated term') to die.

43/4 intercessors: the pagans regard their idols (identified with angels) as intercessors on their behalf with the supreme God.

44/5 belongs intercession: that is, he gives permission to intercede with him.

49/50 – 59/60 Men's attitudes to God

49/50 because of a knowledge: either because of my wisdom, or because God knows my deserts; in either case good fortune is a 'trial' to test men.

52/3 outspreads and straitens: see comment on 13.26.

53/4 prodigal: lacking restraint, and so sinning.

60/1 – 74 God as judge

61/2 in their security: probably means by allowing them to escape punishment.

65 if thou associatest . . .: this is encouragement to Muḥammad to resist Meccan attempts at compromise.

69 the Book: probably the record of men's deeds; but it might be the original of the revealed scriptures, since the next words speak of the issue between the prophets and their opponents.

40

THE BELIEVER

Al-Mu'min

Mainly late Meccan. The sura is also known as 'The Forgiver' (*al-ghāfir*).

1 – 6 God's mercy and power

5 *the parties:* perhaps 'heathen peoples'; cf. 38.11/10 and v. 31/2 below.

7 – 9 Intercession for believers

7 *those who bear the Throne:* angels.

10 – 22/3 God's judgements

12 *was called to alone:* the commentators understood this as disbelieving when it was proclaimed that God is one.

23/4 – 50/3 Moses and Pharaoh

28/9 *prodigal:* also in vv. 34/6, 43/6; see comment on 39.53/4.

32/4 the Day of Invocation: that is, Judgement Day, because believers and unbelievers will call to one another.

36/8 the cords: see comment on 38.10/9.

51/4 – 68/70 God's support, guidance and other acts of mercy

56/8 without any authority . . .: that is, they oppose the signs without having received any authority (from God) for an alternative.

is only pride . . .: or 'greatness beyond their reach'.

69/71 – 85 The unbelievers and God's signs

77 be thou patient: addressed to Muḥammad, who is to believe that God will punish the wicked even if he (Muḥammad) dies first.

78 to bring a sign: sc. a miracle to confirm the truth of his message.

79 cattle: see comment on 36.71.

41
DISTINGUISHED
Fuṣṣilat

Meccan; also known as 'Prostration' (*sajda*).

1 – 8/7 Messenger and message

3/2 *distinguished:* perhaps 'clearly expressed'; the 'signs' here are presumably verses; the words 'an Arabic Koran' are not necessarily to be taken with 'distinguished'.

5/4 *so act:* sc. 'as you think right; and we shall act as we think right'.

9/8 – 18/17 God's power in creation

9/8 *in two days:* perhaps to be identified with the third and fourth days in *Genesis*, 1.9–19.

10/9 *in four days:* plants were created on the third day, animals of sea and air on the fifth, mammals and man on the sixth (cf. *Genesis*, 1.20–31).

equal to those who ask: this is taken to mean that each receives what it requires; or perhaps it means 'this is an easy calculation for those who ask questions'.

11/10 *smoke:* probably intended to describe the formless darkness of *Genesis*, I.2; this verse and the next correspond to the first two days of creation in *Genesis*.

12/11 and to preserve: sc. from demons; cf. 37.6 f.

14/13 from before them and from behind them: this may perhaps be understood of time, namely 'when the Messengers came to various people before and after Ad and Thamood'.

19/18 – 36 Judgement on unbelievers and believers

24/3 if they ask amends . . .: the point of this is not clear.

25/4 comrades: that is, demons.

26/5 and talk idly: or 'but talk idly'; probably meaning 'criticize it', or perhaps 'chatter while it is being recited'.

37 – 40 God's signs

39 thou seest the earth humble: that is, with its vegetation withered and no life on it.

41 – 54 The message to Muḥammad and Moses, etc

43 naught is said to thee . . .: this is an assertion of the essential identity of the revelation to Muḥammad with previous revelations.

44 barbarous: that is, non-Arabic.

its signs not distinguished: that is, its verses not clearly expressed.

called: that is, called to or addressed from such a distance that they cannot hear what is said.

45 *a Word that preceded:* the decision to leave the dispute to be settled at the Day of Judgement.

47 *there is not a witness among us:* the unbelievers are speaking, and the meaning probably is that none can give a proof of the truth of their previous belief in idols.

will think: that is, perceive.

52 *If it is from God . . .:* if the Qur'ān is from God and you disbelieve in it, you are in serious error.

53 *in the horizons:* possibly meant signs connected with the sun and stars; but it is often taken to mean 'in the wide earth' and as referring to later Muslim victories.

42
COUNSEL
Ash-shūrā

Late Meccan or early Medinan.

1 – 12/10 God's glory, His revelation and His purpose

5/3 *the heavens wellnigh are rent . . .: sc.* at the sound of the angels' praises; or before his majesty and glory.

7/5 *the Mother of Cities:* Mecca; if the verse was revealed at Medina, the people of the latter would be included in 'those who dwell about it'; there is no mention of contact between Muḥammad and neighbouring tribes before the Hijra.

13/11 – 18/17 Muḥammad and various opponents

13/11 *scatter not:* do not split up into sects or parties; so also 'scattered not' in v. 14/13.

14/13 *until a stated term: sc.* deferring it until . . .

15/14 *I believe in whatever Book . . .:* this attitude is modified by some Muslims in the light of the assertion that the Books actually in the hands of Jews and Christians have been corrupted.

17/16 the Balance: perhaps the laws laid down in the Qur'ān, or perhaps a symbol of justice.

19/18 – 35/3 God's goodness, especially to believers

21/0 the Word of Decision: said to imply 'that gave them respite'.

23/2 except love for the kinsfolk: perhaps means good treatment for Muḥammad's family; or it could be translated 'except love such as is shown among kinsfolk'.

36/4 – 48/7 The fate of believers and unbelievers

38/6 their affair being counsel between them: perhaps simply 'and (who) counsel one another'.

39/7 help themselves: defend themselves.

40/38 his wage falls upon God: God is responsible for rewarding him.

41/39 helps himself: that is, himself acts in retaliation; the *lex talionis* is thus accepted in Islam, and action in accordance with it will not be reckoned a sin; but forgiveness, when one has been injured, is commended.

49/8 – 53 God's omnipotence; the nature of revelation

51/0 revelation: this seems to indicate here not revelation in general, but some particular 'manner of revelation'; the following phrases indicate other 'manners'; 'from behind a veil' implies hearing words without seeing anything, whereas 'a messenger' implies some vision of a figure.

52 *a Spirit of Our bidding:* 'bidding' (*amr*) may also be translated 'affair'; there is something to be said for the view that *amr* represents the *memra* or *logos* of God.

43
ORNAMENTS
Az-zukhruf

Mostly from the middle Meccan period.

1 – 8/7 The Arabic Book; the penalty of unbelief

4/3 the Essence of the Book: literally 'mother of the book'; the heavenly original that is with God.

8/7 stronger ... than they: sc. than Muḥammad's contemporaries who disbelieved in him.
the example of the ancients passed away: that is, the ancients received exemplary punishment, and this actually happened in the past.

9/8 – 25/4 The unbelievers and their numerous deities

15/14 have assigned to Him: presumably implying 'as offspring'.

17/16 tidings of that he has likened ...: the expression is awkward, but the general sense is 'news of the birth of a daughter'.

18/17 what, one who is reared ...: is such a person good enough for God'.

22/1 upon a community: or 'going in a certain direction in religious matters'.

26/5 – 45/4 Opposition to Abraham and Muhammad

31/0 the two cities: usually taken to be Mecca and aṭ-Ṭā-'if.

33/2 would be one nation: sc. of unbelievers.

37/6 they bar them: that is, the Satans bar the unbelievers.

38/7 the distance of the two Easts: that is, the distance of the east from the west.

44/3 questioned: sc. about obedience to God's commands.

46/5 – 56 Moses and Pharaoh

48/7 its sister sign: probably means 'the one before it'; the reference is to the plagues, as is also that in 'chastisement'.

54 made his people unsteady: the precise sense is not clear, but it probably means 'led them astray'.

57 – 66 Jesus; objections by pagans (?) and Jews

57 thy people turn away: probably refers to the pagan Meccans, who would be afraid of the political implications of Christianity, namely, alliance with the Byzantines or Ethiopians.

61 it is knowledge: presumably 'the Qur'ān'; a variant reading and interpretation are 'he (Jesus) is a sign (*'alam*) of the Hour' (since he is expected to return before then).

67 – 80 The Judgement

77 Malik: usually taken to be the chief angel-guard of Hell.

81 – 9 God has no child nor peer

82 Glory be . . . above . . .: Ar. *subḥān Allāh . . . 'an*; the words *subḥān Allāh* are normally translated 'Glory be to God', but the more exact meaning of *subḥān* is 'the declaring (God) to be far removed from, or above, all imperfection'; here it means he is far removed from having offspring.

83 to plunge: to occupy themselves, *sc.* with vanity.

44
SMOKE
Ad-dukhān

Middle Meccan Period.

1 – 16/15 The Book as warning; the punishment

3/2 in a blessed night: sc. the Night of Power in 97.1.

4/3 therein every wise bidding determined: or 'in (that night) every wise matter is decided'; *sc* .matter whose decision requires wisdom.

5/4 as a bidding from us: or '(The Book is sent) as a matter (coming) from us'; the precise point of the verse is obscure.

9/8 a manifest smoke: some scholars say this was a strange smoke which filled the air at Mecca during a famine; others take it as a sign that the day of judgement is imminent.

14/13 tutored: sc. being given information; cf. 16.103/5.

17/16 – 33/2 Pharaoh and the Children of Israel

17/16 a noble Messenger: sc. Moses; though the name is not mentioned, there is nothing inconsistent with the story of Moses.

24/3 becalmed: or 'divided'.

31/0 prodigals: sc. transgressors.

32/1 chose them, out of a knowledge: sc. the Children of Israel, either knowing they were worthy to be chosen or knowing they would fall into sin.

34/3 – 42 The Resurrection doubted

37/6 Tubba: the title of the kings of the Ḥimyarites in South Arabia.

43 – 50 The punishment of Hell

43 Ez-Zakkoum: Ar. az-Zaqqūm; a tree in Hell.

51 – 9 The reward of Paradise

58 have made it easy: sc. the Qur'ān.

45
HOBBLING
Al-jāthiya

Late Meccan, but a few verses may be Medinan.

1 – 13/12 God's signs

6/5 after God and His signs: sc. after they have heard and rejected God's signs or verses, is there any kind of communication they will accept?

14/13 – 15/14 The days of God

14/13 the days of God: perhaps the days when God punishes supernaturally (as in 14.5); but usually taken to mean victories like that at Badr; these verses are then said to have been revealed in connection with the expedition against Banū Muṣṭaliq.

16/15 – 26/5 Various forms of disobedience and unbelief

24/3 nothing but Time destroys us: Ar. *dahr*; the common view of the pagan Arabs was that death and misfortune were brought to men by 'time' or 'the days', which are roughly the same as 'fate'.

27/6 – 37/6 Judgement

28/7 hobbling on their knees: or simply 'kneeling' but with the suggestion of expecting something, and here it is the judgement they are waiting for.

every nation being summoned unto its Book: the Book may be its revealed scripture since 'nation' (*umma*) connotes a community following a simple religion; or it may be the record of men's deeds as in the next verse.

46

THE SAND-DUNES

Al-aḥqāf

Late Meccan with some Medinan verses.

1–12/11 Appeals to unbelievers regarding idols, and the Qur'ān

3/2 save with the truth: probably meaning 'with a serious purpose and not in sport'; cf. 21.16; 38.27/6; the word 'truth' (*ḥaqq*), however, also suggests 'judgement', and the following words, 'a stated term', imply that the heavens and the earth will come to an end before the Day of Judgement (cf. 30.8/7).

4/3 some remnant of a knowledge: probably means some record or anecdote of what was known in a previous age.

8/7 are pressing upon: or 'are engaged in'.

9/8 not an innovation: or 'not the first of ...'.

10/9 a witness: usually said to have been a Jew, 'Abd-Allāh ibn-Salām, who declared Muḥammad was the prophet foretold in *Deuteronomy*; perhaps, however, the witness is rather Moses himself.

13/12–20/19 The righteous; attitudes to parents

15/14 reaches forty years: the conventional age of maturity.

17/16 brought forth: sc. from the grave.

19/18 their degrees: sc. of happiness or misery; or 'their ranks (in heaven)'.

21/0 – 28/7 The people of 'Ād

26/5 had established them . . .: sc. had given them greater power and authority than you Meccans.

27/6 the cities about you: the precise reference is obscure; the following 'they' probably means the inhabitants of the cities.

29/8 – 32/1 Jinn believe in the Qur'ān

29/8 a company of jinn: these invisible beings are regarded as being capable of responding to God's message or failing to respond and so of meriting Paradise or Hell; an incident in which jinn were converted at Muḥammad's preaching, is said to have occurred at Nakhla on his return from aṭ-Ṭā'if in 619 or 620.

33/2 – 35 Resurrection and Judgement

35 tarried: sc. in the grave; or the reference may be to the whole of their earthly life compared with eternity.

47

MUHAMMAD

Muḥammad

Revealed at Medina about the time of the battle of Badr (624).

1 – 3 God's dealings with believers and unbelievers

3 *their similitudes: sc.* to instruct them; or it may mean 'God shows the people their essence, or what they are like'.

4 – 15/17 War with Mecca; God is with the believers

4 *tie fast the bonds:* make them prisoners.

4/5 *avenged Himself:* would have punished them directly, not through human intermediaries.

16/18 – 38/40 Reluctance to believe, and especially to fight

16/18 *those who have been given knowledge:* Muḥammad's convinced followers.

17/19 *gives them their godfearing: sc.* makes them more godfearing.

18/20 *its tokens have come:* or 'the conditions for it . . .'; may refer to the smoke of sura 44 or to such matters as the rejection of Muḥammad.

20/2 swoons of death: sc. at the fear or agony of death.

22/4 break your bonds of kin: sc. by shedding kinsmen's blood.

26/8 those who were averse . . .: perhaps 'Abd-Allāh ibn-Ubayy or some of the Jews in alliance with him.

31/3 try your tidings: sc. reports of your behaviour.

38/40 will not be your likes: sc. but will respond to God's message.

48
VICTORY
Al-fat'ḥ

Revealed about the time of the expedition to al-Ḥudaybiya in March 628. Muḥammad in a dream had seen himself performing the pilgrimage rites with his followers. When, however, with about 1,600 men and their sacrificial victims, he approached Mecca, the Meccans barred his way. He halted at al-Ḥudaybiya on the edge of the sacred territory of Mecca, and eventually a treaty with the Meccans was signed, by which the Muslims agreed to retire for that year but were allowed to perform the pilgrimage in the next year. To many of Muḥammad's followers this may have seemed a defeat, but the Meccans had in fact recognized him as a person with whom they made treaties on equal terms. Cf. *Medina*, 46–52.

1 – 10 Assurances to Muḥammad

1 a manifest victory: traditionally this was often taken as referring to the conquest of Mecca in January 630; sometimes it was held that, though the passage was revealed on the way back from al-Ḥudaybiya, it referred proleptically to the conquest as past, since it was virtually certain. It could also be said that the treaty was a victory in itself, since after it the surrender of Mecca was just a matter of time. Another possibility is to take the word *fat'ḥ* literally as 'opening'; and it certainly opened the way to the conquest of Mecca.

2 thy former and thy latter sins: possibly means those in the Jāhiliyya and those afterwards.

4 Shechina: or 'assurance'; cf. comment on 2.248/9. Whatever the precise nature of the experience, it must have been connected with the Muslims' acceptance of the outcome of the expedition despite their disappointment at not performing the pilgrimage rites.

6 the Hypocrites: almost certainly not the followers of 'Abd-Allāh ibn-Ubayy, for he took full part in the expedition to al-Ḥudaybiya and was reconciled to Muḥammad; the words must refer to the later group connected with 'the mosque of dissension'.

8 We have sent thee as a witness: perhaps this assurance to Muḥammad was to counteract the fact that his dream had not been realized.

10 swear fealty to thee: Ar. *yubāyi'ūn*; or 'do homage' or 'acknowledge'; the word was later used of the popular acclamation of a new caliph. The reference here is probably to the Pledge under the Tree, a pledge to obey Muḥammad to the death, taken by the Muslims when the situation appeared grave (*Medina*, 50); see comment on v. 18.

11 – 17 Criticisms of the Bedouins

11 who were left behind . . .: Muḥammad had expected that most of the allied nomadic tribes near Medina would join in the expedition, but they had all made excuses; they were probably still afraid of the Meccans (cf. v. 12), and saw little prospect of booty.

if He desires hurt for you: that is, if God has willed that you should be hurt, you cannot avoid it by staying away from dangerous situations.

12 that was decked out fair: that is, if Muḥammad and his followers had been killed, the Bedouins would have been delighted, for they were not religious, and probably found Muḥammad's rule irksome.

15 *when you set forth after spoils:* this refers to the (forthcoming) expedition to Khaybar; eventually (perhaps on the basis of this verse) only those who had gone to al-Ḥudaybiya were allowed to take part.

16 *shall be called against . . .:* probably refers to the expedition to Mu'ta in September 629 against the tribe of Ghassān.

or they surrender: that is, 'unless they first surrender'; the word 'surrender' (*yuslimūn*) could mean 'become Muslims' but almost certainly does not mean that here, since the expedition was against Christian tribes who would normally be offered the status of 'protected person' (*dhimmī*).

turned your backs before: sc. in not going to al-Ḥudaybiya.

17 *no fault in the blind: sc.* for not taking part in expeditions.

18 *well pleased:* presumably because of this word (*raḍiya*) the pledge at al-Ḥudaybiya is known as 'the pledge of good pleasure' (*bay'at ar-riḍwān*); it is also known from the following words as 'the pledge under the tree'.

a nigh victory: either near at hand (perhaps with the thought of Khaybar) or in the near future; rich spoils were in fact obtained from the Jewish oasis of Khaybar in May and June 628. Cf. v. 27.

20 *these He has hastened to you:* probably the spoils of Khaybar, whereas the 'other spoils' below might be those of Mecca which they did not get.

restrained the hands of men: means they were not attacked on the expedition to al-Ḥudaybiya.

22 *if the unbelievers had fought you: sc.* the Meccans.

24 *made you victors:* Ar. *aẓfara-kum*; this is the accepted rendering, but it is difficult to understand which victory can be referred to; the translation 'made you successful' might be suggested, with the interpretation that the treaty negotiations were to be regarded as a Muslim success.

25 *and the offering, detained . . .:* that is, barred both you and the offering (of animals, and it was) detained.

lest you should trample them: that is, had there been fighting leading to a conquest of Mecca, some Muslim men and women, residing in Mecca but unknown to Muḥammad, might have been injured, and the Muslims would have incurred guilt; but God did not allow this to happen.

26 *set in their hearts fierceness:* this is said to refer to the period when the Meccan representatives were making difficulties about the wording of the treaty, e.g. refusing to allow the phrase 'Messenger of God'.

27 *has fulfilled the vision:* presumably, if revealed shortly after the treaty, means that God has fulfilled the vision by the treaty permitting the pilgrimage in the following year.

your heads shaved . . .: marks of the pilgrims.

29 *in the Torah:* God's words are 'as frontlets between your eyes' (*Deuteronomy,* 11.18, cf. 6.8).

in the Gospel: cf. *Mark,* 4.26–9 (seed cast in the ground), 30–2 (mustard seed).

49

APARTMENTS

Al-ḥujurāt

Revealed a year or two before Muḥammad's death.

1 – 5 Behaviour of Muslims towards Muḥammad

1 advance not: do not be first with proposals; or perhaps do not exaggerate your importance.

2 raise not your voices: this and the following verses (and perhaps the preceding one) are said to have been revealed in 630 or 631 after a deputation from the tribe of Tamīm, dealing with the freeing of prisoners, shouted and made a noise because Muḥammad did not come to them immediately.

lest your works fail: probably means 'lest, by so acting, you fail to achieve your object'.

4 from behind the apartments: while Muḥammad is in the apartments of his wives (each wife had a separate room or suite), they call to him from outside and expect him to go out.

6 – 13 Mutual relations of believers

6 make clear: test the report; this verse and the next two are said to have been revealed about 630 when al-Walīd ibn-'Uqba reported that the tribe of Muṣṭaliq had refused to give their tax payment to him, and had threatened his life; before any reprisals had been taken, Muḥammad discovered that they had not in fact refused, but that al-Walīd had withdrawn in fear; the word *fāsiq* ('ungodly' or 'evil'), however, seems to be too strong to be applied to him.

9 *if two parties of the believers fight* . . .: this is said to refer to a quarrel between 'Abd-Allāh ibn-Ubayy and 'Abd-Allāh ibn-Rawāḥa and their followers; but such a quarrel seems unlikely at any date near that of the rest of the sura.

11 *neither let women scoff* . . .: this is said to have been revealed because other women had scoffed at one of Muḥammad's wives (Ṣafiyya) because she was a Jewess; Muḥammad is said to have told her to retort 'Aaron is my father, Moses my uncle, and Muḥammad my husband'.

14 – 18 Criticism of Bedouin Arabs

14 *We surrender:* Ar. *aslamnā,* which can mean 'we have become Muslims'; but most commentators reject this meaning here since it implies an untenable distinction between 'believers' and 'Muslims', and say the word is equivalent to *iṣtaslamnā,* 'we have sought peace by submission'. The occasion of the revelation of the passage is said to have been the profession of Islam by bedouin of the tribe of Asad ibn-Khuzayma in order to be fed by Muḥammad in a time of famine (probably 631). It is less likely to refer specifically to those who refused to join the expedition to al-Ḥudaybiya.

15 *struggled:* that is, 'fought'.

16 *would you teach God* . . .?: that is, make out that your religion is different from what it really is.

17 *they count it a favour* . . .: the bedouin think they are doing Muḥammad a favour by becoming Muslims.

50
QĀF
Qāf

Middle or late Meccan period.

1 – 14 Replies to unbelievers about God's power and goodness

4 what the earth diminishes of them: sc. how bodies moulder in the grave.

8 servant: sc. of God; that is, man; cf. v. 11 below.

15 – 37/6 Death, judgement and recompense

15 the two angels: it is usually said that the angel on the right records good actions and the angel on the left bad actions.

20 a driver and a witness: one (perhaps the angel of death) hales him before the tribunal, while the other gives an account of his good and bad deeds; this is not altogether consistent with the usual interpretation of v. 15.

21 covering: probably meaning veil.

26 his comrade: a devil attached to each man; cf. 43.36/5.

38/7 – 45 Muḥammad to be patient and praise God

39/8 be thou patient under what they say: presumably the denial of resurrection and other objections of pagans.

44/3 the earth is split asunder . . .: that is, the graves are opened.

51
THE SCATTERERS
Adh-dhariyāt

Probably middle Meccan period for the most part.

1 – 6 Judgement is certainly imminent

1 the swift scatterers: this and the following verses have a participle in the feminine plural as keyword; the precise reference can only be guessed; for this the winds scattering dust have been suggested, or women giving birth to children.

2 the burden-bearers: winds bringing clouds and rain; or pregnant women.

3 the smooth runners: ships, or winds, or stars.

4 the partitioners: winds or angels.

7 – 23 Doubters; Paradise; God is true

8 speak at variance: express different views, probably about the Qur'ān.

24 – 37 Abraham

24 honoured guests: cf. *Genesis*, 18.

26 his household: sc. wife, primarily.

28 conceived a fear: because they did not eat; cf. 11.70/3.

a cunning boy: or 'wise' or 'prudent'.

38 – 40 Moses

41 – 46 Unbelieving peoples

44 and they themselves beholding: sc. as they looked.

47 – 60 God's power and justice

48 smothers: apparently God Himself.

52

THE MOUNT

Aṭ-ṭūr

Fairly early Meccan.

1 – 8 God's punishment certain

1 *the Mount: sc.* Sinai; in accordance with this 'the Book' in v. 2 is probably the law given there to Moses.

4 *the House inhabited:* that is, thronged with people; or 'visited' *sc.* by pilgrims; in either case the reference is to the Ka'ba.

5 *the roof:* probably the sky.

6 *swarming:* or perhaps 'swelling'.

9 – 28 Hell and Paradise

12 *at plunging: sc.* into vain disputes.

21 *shall be pledged for what he earned:* that is, each is liable to the reward or punishment for his deeds.

24 *their own: sc.* servants or attendants; they are as handsome as hidden pearls.

29 – 49 Muḥammad and the unbelievers

30 *Fate's uncertainty:* that is, some disaster.

33 *has invented it: sc.* the Qur'ān.

38 *a ladder: sc.* to heaven, so that they may hear what is said in council.

40 *askest thou . . . for a wage?:* 'do you, Muḥammad, ask to be paid for delivering God's messages?'

44 *lumps: sc.* a fragment of the sky.

53
THE STAR
An-najm

Probably part the early and part the middle Meccan period, with at least one verse from Medina.

1–18 Muḥammad's truthfulness supported by two visions

2 your comrade: Muḥammad; the Meccans are addressed.

3 nor speaks he out of caprice: he is not telling something based merely on personal inclination.

5 one terrible in power: usually taken to be the angel Gabriel; but the words 'to his servant' (*ilā 'abdi-hi*) in v. 10 can only mean 'to God's servant'; it may thus be the case that this was originally taken to be a vision of God, until it was learned that God cannot be seen in this life.

11 his heart lies not: that is, does not falsely represent what he saw, so that he is not deceiving himself.

14, 15 the lote-tree ... the Garden ...: probably places in the region of Mecca, but commentators have often taken them to be celestial.

19–30/1 The pagan goddesses

19, 20 El-Lat ... El-'Uzza ... Manat: these goddesses were specially connected with three shrines in the neighbourhood of Mecca, namely at aṭ-Ṭā'if, Nakhla (on the road to aṭ-Ṭā'if), and at a place on the road to Medina. The story is that when these verses were first recited, Muḥammad was anxious to win over the pagan Meccans, and failed to notice when Satan introduced two (or three) further verses permitting intercession at these shrines. This story could hardly have been invented, and gains support from sura 22, v. 52/1 (see comment). At length Muḥammad realized the substitution, and received the continuing revelation as it now is in the Qur'ān.

22 an unjust division: it would be unjust, if God had only daughters, whereas men had sons (as well as daughters). The idols mentioned were known as 'daughters of God', though this did not imply a family system, as in Greek mythology, but only that these were (in the eyes of those who used the phrase) divine beings of a sort, subordinate to God.

23 naught but names: this is the most extreme criticism of paganism in the Qur'ān, denying all reality to the pagan deities; elsewhere (as in v. 26) it is allowed that some of them may be angels, though this still does not make it permissible to worship them.

24 shall man have whatever he fancies?: that is, will he determine the conditions of his life and the nature of his religion?

26 whose intercession avails not anything, save . . .: intercession by angels is possible by God's permission, but would obviously not be available for those who mistakenly regarded the angels as divine (as in v. 27/8).

29/30 turn thou from him . . .: Muḥammad is to break his relationship with the pagans, and not consider any compromise.

31/2 – 62 God punishes and forgives

33/4 him who turns his back . . .: sc. on the revealed message;

this and the following are probably to be understood generally of the attitude of the rich Meccan merchants; some scholars, however, have referred particularly to al-Walīd ibn-al-Mughīra who is alleged to have given up following Muḥammad when, for a financial consideration, another man said he would take on himself the guilt of al-Walīd's apostasy; in due course al-Walīd paid him some of the money, but not all.

37/8 who paid his debt in full: or 'who fulfilled his engagements'.

47/8 rests the second growth: that is, rests the obligation to give men life a second time at the resurrection.

49/50 the lord of Sirius: the star Sirius (the dog-star) was worshipped by some pagan Arabs.

53/4 the Subverted City: Sodom and its region.

54
THE MOON
Al-qamar

Middle Meccan period.

1 – 8 The Last Day is near

1 the moon is split: this was a sign of the Last Day, and the assertion here that it has happened, may indicate certainty or imminence; many Muslim scholars, however, interpreted the verse of a miracle God performed for Muḥammad, in which the moon was actually seen split in two.

4 such tidings: sc. in the Qur'ān.

6 the Caller: the angel summoning men to Judgement.

9 – 17 Noah

14 before Our eyes: that is, God watched over him.

for him denied: for the one who had been rejected.

15 left it for a sign: probably the story, not the ship.

18 – 32 Ad and Thamood

31 pen-builder: making a pen for cattle.

33 – 42 The people of Lot; Pharaoh

34 *the folk of Lot:* or 'family' (also in v. 41).

37 *we obliterated their eyes:* some Muslim scholars say that the eyes were miraculously removed and the sockets filled up; but it is more likely the words were taken metaphorically.

43 – 55 Warning to the Meccans

48 *Sakar:* Ar. Saqar; a proper name of Hell, suggesting 'scorching'.

50 *Our commandment is but one word:* or 'our affair is but one act'; the reference in either case is to the Judgement.

55

THE ALL-MERCIFUL

Ar-Raḥmān

Probably Meccan. A distinctive feature of this sura is the refrain or antiphon ('O which of your Lord's bounties . . .') repeated 31 times.

1 – 32 God's goodness in the heavens and the earth

4/3 *the Explanation: sc.* of the Qur'ān.

5/4 *to a reckoning:* means either 'serve man for reckoning time' or 'have a regular, calculable movement'.

13/12 *you and you:* the Arabic dual is used, possibly referring to men and jinn.

17/16 *the two Easts:* said to mean the point of sunrise at the winter and summer solstices; similarly for the 'two Wests'.

19 *the two seas:* cf. comment on 35.12/13.

28 *whatsoever is . . . implore him:* that is, all who are in the heavens and the earth make requests to him.

upon some labour: that is, has something to do; the commentators say it is in fulfilment of what He has eternally decreed.

31 *you weight and you weight:* that is, you two burdensome companies, *sc.* of men and jinn.

33 – 45 The punishment of sin and ingratitude

33 *pass through the confines:* that is, go beyond them out of the reach of God.

39 *none will be questioned: sc.* because the nature of the sin will be evident from the mark.

46 – 78 The reward of the god-fearing

46 *the Station of his Lord:* perhaps His judgement-seat, or perhaps merely 'fears his Lord'.

two gardens: perhaps for men and jinn; but the reason for two is not clear.

76 *druggets:* the Arabic *'abqarī* means a type of rich carpet.

56
THE TERROR
Al-wāqiʿa

Probably early Meccan, except that a few verses may be Medinan.

1 – 9 The coming of Judgement

1 *the Terror:* that is, the sudden calamity marking the Day of Judgement.

7 *three bands:* apparently those on the right, those on the left, and the 'outstrippers'.

10 – 26/5 The first band—those in bliss

10 *the Outstrippers:* Ar. *sābiqūn*; either the first converts to Islam or persons outstanding for their religious and moral qualities.

11 *brought nigh the Throne:* the words 'the Throne' are not in the Arabic, but something like this must be assumed; cf. comment on 26.42/1; also 40.7.

19 *brows throbbing:* with a headache.

23/2 *for that they laboured:* that is, for what they did in their earthly life.

27/6 – 40/39 The second band—those on the Right

40/39 a throng of the later folk: this is in contrast to 'few of the later folk' in v. 14; apart from this it is not clear how the Companions of the Right differ from the first band.

41/0 – 56 The third band—those on the Left

46/5 the Great Sin: that is, unbelief; more exactly it is the failure to perform their obligation of acknowledging God.

57 – 74/3 God's power

60 not to be outstripped: that is, 'men cannot run so quickly as to outrun Us and escape death, or prevent Us from exchanging . . .'.

61 exchange the likes of you: probably means 'substitute others for you'.

64 sow: in the sense of bringing about the whole development of the seed till it is ripe for harvest.

65 broken orts: sc. vegetation dried up and broken.

67/6 we have been robbed: sc. of success and the expected result of our labours.

75/4 – 97/6 The nobility of the Qur'ān

78/7 in a hidden Book: perhaps the original in heaven.

82/1 make it your living to cry lies: probably means 'make it your custom to declare the Qur'ān false'.

86/5 why, if you are not . . .: that is, 'why, if you human beings are not liable to God's judgement, do you not restore the man to life?' It is implied that to be exempt from judgement includes having power over life and death; or that to restore to life is easier than escaping judgement.

57
IRON
Al-ḥadīd

Probably from the first two or three years at Medina.

1 – 6 The glory of God

2 the Outward and the Inward: Ar. *ẓāhir, bāṭin*; may also mean 'the manifest and the hidden'.

6 to enter into the day: that is, to pass over into the day; and similarly in the following clause.

7 – 11 Appeal for belief and contributions

7 successors: or 'inheritors'.

9 clear signs: that is, the verses of the Qur'ān.

His servant: sc. Muḥammad.

10 you expend not in the way of God: that is, you do not give contributions to Muḥammad for the work of the community of Muslims.

who spent and who fought before the victory: the victory (Ar. *fat'ḥ*) is probably the conquest of Mecca, and in some versions of the Dīwān or system of stipends those who had become

Muslims before the conquest of Mecca had a special place; for another possible meaning of *fat'ḥ*, see comment on 32.28.

11 lend to God a good loan: by doing good acts, or more particularly by contributing money.

12 – 24 Believers, hypocrites and unbelievers

12 their light . . .: it is sometimes said that the light running before them is one guiding them to Paradise, while that on their right hands comes from the book recording their good deeds which is in their right hands.

13 a wall . . . having a door . . .: that is, on the inner side of these, where the believers are, is mercy, and on the outer side punishment.

14/13 you awaited: sc. (probably) hoping that some misfortune would overtake Muḥammad and the Muslims.

God's commandment: cf. comment on 54.50.

16/15 the term: Ar. *amad, sc.* the time they had to wait for God's deliverance.

19/18 martyrs: Ar. *shuhadā'*; those who have died fighting 'in the way of God' or otherwise active in it.

21 race to forgiveness: sc. vie with one another in seeking it.

23 for what escapes you: sc. good that has not been given to you.

what has come to you: that is, they are not to rejoice as if their possessions came through their own activity.

25 – 29 Messengers and their followers

25 *sent down iron:* that is, taught men how to find the ore and manufacture it.

26 *some of them . . . many of them:* of their seed or their followers.

27 *only seeking the pleasure . . .: sc.* they invented monasticism in their strong desire to be pleasing to God.

58
THE DISPUTER
Al-mujādila

Revealed at Medina, probably at different times.

1 – 6/7 The formula of divorce

1 her that disputes: said to be Khawla bint-Tha'laba, wife of Aws ibn-aṣ-Ṣāmit, who divorced her by the pagan formula, 'Be to me as my mother's back'; and then regretted his step. When Muḥammad was appealed to, he at first said the divorce was valid, but afterwards received this revelation. Later scholars dated it about the time of al-Ḥudaybiya (628 AD).

3/4 retract what they have said: this seems to be the correct translation, though it is disputed; the point is that the formula made any further sexual intercourse between the pair incestuous, and so an act of atonement was necessary; cf. 33.4.

7/8 – 13/14 Various points concerning relationships among Muslims

7/8 three men conspire . . .: such conspiracies and secret conclaves might belong to the period when 'Abd-Allāh ibn-Ubayy and the Hypocrites were actively opposing Muḥammad; but it is more likely that they belong to the time of the 'Mosque of Dissension' (late 630).

8/9 greet thee with a greeting: it is said that for *as-salām 'alay-k* (peace to you), they substituted *as-sām 'alay-k* (death to you); they then argued that, if Muḥammad were a prophet, God would punish them for this.

12/13 when you conspire with the Messenger: the word is from the same root as in v. 7/8, but the connotation here is 'speak privately'.

advance a freewill offering: present an alms; this verse is held to be abrogated by the following.

13/14 then perform the prayer . . .: that is, at least do this.

14/15 – 22 Counsels about making friends

14/15 those who have taken for friends . . .: these are usually said to be Hypocrites, who had friendly relations with Jews; but it is possible that the reference is to the Hypocrites connected with the Mosque of Dissension, since one of the builders of this, 'Abd-Allāh ibn-Nabtal (Ibn-Hishām, 357), is associated with the latter part of the verse (commentaries of az-Zamakhsharī and al-Bayḍāwī).

59
THE MUSTERING
Al-ḥashr

Revealed at Medina, probably at the time of the expulsion of Banū-n-Naḍīr (August 625).

1–10 The expulsion of the Jews and the distribution of the spoil

2 *at the first mustering:* Ar. *ḥashr;* this is sometimes understood of the act of emigrating, but the first Jews to be expelled were Qaynuqā' in April 624, and on general grounds it is unlikely that these are here intended; probably 'mustering' is to be taken as coming together for punishment, so that 'the first mustering' (for exile) is contrasted with the second on the Last Day.

fortresses: small forts to which one could retire when attacked were a feature of the oasis of Medina.

as they destroyed their houses: this is said to refer to the fact that, after they had surrendered and agreed to leave Medina, they tore the lintels from their houses to carry with them.

4 *made a breach with:* perhaps no more than 'opposed'; the story in the biography of Muḥammad is that they tried to kill him by dropping a large stone on him while he sat with his back resting on one of their houses discussing a question of blood-money.

5 *whatever palm trees . . .:* an-Naḍir surrendered when they saw

the Muslims cutting down their palms; this was regarded as an underhand practice, but the Arabic word *līna* is said to exclude the best kind of palms.

6 against that you pricked . . .: an-Naḍīr did not yield to an attack, but surrendered when they saw the palm-trees being destroyed.

7 the near kinsman, orphans . . .: this verse restricts the distribution of spoil to the classes mentioned; 'the near kinsmen' are probably mentioned because Muḥammad had a special obligation to look after Muslims of his own clan.

8 is for the poor emigrants: sc. the Muslims who had gone with Muḥammad from Mecca to Medina; since the lands of an-Naḍīr were in fact given to poor Emigrants (and two poor Muslims of Medina), it would seem that this verse must be taken closely with v. 6, while v. 7 may give a later and more general regulation.

9 in the abode: presumably Medina, so that the whole phrase indicates the Muslims of Medina who must in the early days have been generous in their hospitality to the Emigrants.

10 those who came after them: later Emigrants from Mecca.

11 – 17 The Hypocrites lack courage

11 we will go forth with you: this probably refers to 'Abd-Allāh ibn-Ubayy and his party; they presumably meant that they would resist expulsion as vigorously as if they themselves were to be expelled; actually it soon became evident that these hypocrites had not sufficient power to organize resistance to Muḥammad.

14 you arouse . . .: that is, you Muslims.

15 those who a short time before them . . .: either the Jewish clan of Qaynuqāʿ or the Meccans killed at Badr.

18 – 24 Exhortation to fear God

18 for the morrow: the Day of Judgement.

24 the Names Most Beautiful: the Names of God (sometimes said to be 99, though there are more) play an important part in Muslim thought and worship; cf. *EI*², art. ʻal-Asmāʼ al-Ḥusnāʼ (Louis Gardet); cf. 7.180/79.

60

THE WOMAN TESTED

Al mumtaḥana

Revealed at Medina between the treaty of al-Ḥudaybiya (March 628) and the conquest of Mecca (January 630).

1 – 9 Treatment of enemies

1 take not My enemy . . . for friends: this is said to have been revealed in connection with a man called Ḥāṭib ibn-Abī-Balta'a, a confederate of az-Zubayr from the tribe of Lakhm, who had fought at Badr; when Muḥammad was making preparations for his final assault on Mecca, Ḥāṭib sent a letter to the Meccans by a woman with information, because he wanted his family in Mecca to be well treated; the woman was caught, but he was only reprimanded. The 'enemy' is the Meccan pagans (*Medina,* 112; Ibn-Hishām, 809 f.).

4 I shall ask pardon for thee: cf. 9.113/4 f., where it is noted that this conduct of Abraham was contrary to what was prescribed for Muslims, but was for a special reason and was temporary.

5 make us not a temptation: obscure, perhaps 'do not give them victory so that they tempt us to apostatize'.

7 God will yet establish . . . love: from Muḥammad's actions one may infer that after the failure of the siege of Medina in 627, he was seeking reconciliation with Quraysh; this verse, depending on its date, suggests or confirms this policy.

9 as regards those who have not fought you: this is said to have been revealed when Qutayla bint-'Abd-al-'Uzzā wanted to make a present to her daughter Asmā' (by her former husband Abū-Bakr), and Asmā' refused because Qutayla was still a pagan.

10 – 13 Treatment of women refugees, etc

10 Believing women . . . as emigrants: according to the treaty of al-Ḥudaybiya persons under the protection of another who wanted to become Muslims and join Muḥammad, were to be sent back to their protectors; this is now to be stopped, and women who have become Muslims are not to be given to unbelievers, but the unbelievers must be compensated by what they have expended as dowry.

test them: to ensure they are really believers; hence the name of the sura.

the ties of unbelieving women: unbelieving wives are to be divorced, and what was given as dowry asked back.

let them ask: presumably unbelieving husbands of believing women.

11 then you retaliate: sc. in general, and gain booty, from it give . . .'.

12 upon the terms that . . .: these are quoted as the terms of the Pledge of Women at the first 'Aqaba.

13 a people who have despaired: either infidels or Jews.

61

THE RANKS

Aṣ-ṣaff

Early Medinan of different dates.

2 wherefore do you say what you do not?: this is generally thought to refer to the Muslims who turned and fled at Uḥud; but it may refer to some earlier incident, since most of the rest of the sura seems to be before Badr.

5 when Moses said ...: from here to the end of v. 9 may be taken as a criticism of the Jews of Medina.

6 a Messenger who shall come after me: this is often taken to refer to Jesus' foretelling of the coming of the Paraclete.

whose name shall be Aḥmad: this is sometimes held to rest on a confusion of the Greek *paraklētēs* (comforter, strengthener, advocate) with *perīklutos* (celebrated); the latter is close to Muḥammad (praised) and Aḥmad (more praiseworthy), the latter being accepted as an equivalent of Muḥammad, especially in poetry. It is also possible that we should take *aḥmad* as an adjective—'whose name is more praiseworthy'; Aḥmad was not given as a name to Muslim children until a hundred years after the Hijra (cf. Watt, 'His Name is Aḥmad', *Muslim World*, xliii [1953], 110–17; reprinted in *Early Islam*, Edinburgh University Press, 1990, 43–50).

when he brought them ...: sc. Jesus, cf. 5.110.

13 a nigh victory: most likely this was revealed before Badr.

14 God's helpers: Ar. Anṣār; this eventually became the name of the Medinan Muslims altogether, partly covering over the tension between the Aws and the Khazraj; there is also a play on the Arabic word for 'Christians', Naṣārā.

62

CONGREGATION

Al-jumu'a

Revealed at Medina, some probably early in 624 before the change of Qibla.

1 – 4 Muḥammad sent to the 'common people'

2 common people: Ar. *ummiyyīn,* the Gentiles or non-Jews; that is, more generally, those without written scriptures; cf. comment on 2.78/3.

His signs: or 'verses'.

to purify them: Ar. *yuzakkī*; perhaps implying 'from the uncleanness of paganism'; another possible translation is 'to appoint alms (*zakāt*) for them'; in either case the word is to be taken in a general sense, corresponding to the use of *tazakkā.*

3 others of them: sc. of the 'common people' or Arabs, perhaps referring to nomadic tribes.

5 – 8 The Jews criticized

5 loaded with the Torah: many of the rules specially prescribed for the Jews were considered very burdensome by the Arabs, and in fact had not been observed by the Jews—'they have not carried it'; the ass is not benefited by the books he carries.

6 long for death: since Paradise, of which you are assured, is better; but in fact they are afraid of recompense for their sins ('what their hands have forwarded').

9–11 Worship on Friday

9 the Day of Congregation: Friday, when all Muslims should be present at the midday worship in the chief or 'congregational' mosque (*jāmi'*) of the town.

trafficking: all forms of business.

11 when they see merchandise ....: this is said to have been revealed because on one occasion a caravan of goods arrived at the time of midday worship and all except a dozen of the Muslims left the mosque to look at the caravan.

63

THE HYPOCRITES

Al-munāfiqūn

Verse 8 is said to have been revealed in connection with the expedition against Banū Muṣṭaliq in January 627 (or 628); cf. opening comment on sura 24.

1 the hypocrites: 'Abd-Allāh ibn-Ubayy and his followers.

2 have barred . . .: sc. their fellow-citizens, etc.

4 their bodies: sc. their outward appearance.

propped-up timbers: also said to mean timbers whose centre is wasted or worm-eaten.

7 until they scatter off: that is, so that they leave Medina; the Hypocrites hoped that, if insufficient contributions were given, Muḥammad and the Emigrants would have to abandon Medina.

8 the mightier ones . . . the more abased: that is, we (Hypocrites) will expel Muḥammad and the Muslims from Mecca; these words are held to have been spoken during the expedition against Banū Muṣṭaliq.

10 may make freewill offering: Ar. *aṣṣaddaqa*; perhaps not very different from giving *zakāt*.

64
MUTUAL FRAUD
At-taghābun

Early Medinan, the latter half probably after the battle of Uḥud. The first half is sometimes considered Meccan.

1 – 10 God's glory; the fate of unbelievers

9 the Day of Mutual Fraud: perhaps meaning 'the day on which each party tries to overreach the other', but the precise significance is not clear, except that in some sense the believers may be said to get the better of and overreach the unbelievers.

11 – 18 Trials and temptations of believers

11 no affliction . . .: presumably revealed after the battle of Uḥud, when the Muslims found it difficult to account for the loss of life in the battle.

12 only for the Messenger to deliver . . . .: that is, he is only responsible for delivering the message, not for the attitude of the hearers to it.

14 among your wives and children . . . an enemy: often taken to mean that wife and children distract a man from thoughts of the future life; but the mention of pardon suggests some definite fault, perhaps encouraging their husbands to disobey Muḥammad.

65

DIVORCE

Aṭ-ṭalāq

Probably revealed in the second half of the Medinan period. The regulations for divorce appear to be later than those in 2.228 ff.

1 when you divorce . . .: plural; that is, when you Muslims divorce . . .

have reached their period: Ar. *'idda,* waiting-period for a divorced woman, during which she may not remarry; this passage appears to state that the divorce is not in force until after the waiting-period, but in practice it is only the woman who waits in this way.

will bring something new to pass: that is, there may be some change in the attitude of the man and woman during the waiting-period, and they may be glad that the divorce is not final.

2 perform the witnessing to God: perhaps meaning that it is to be recorded.

4 three months: instead of the three menstrual periods prescribed in 2.228.

6 lodge them: sc. divorced women during their waiting-period.

do not press them . . .: sc. do not make life unbearable for them, so that they have to go elsewhere.

another woman shall suckle: the use of wet-nurses seems to have been common among the Arabs.

12 the Command: Ar. *amr*; here perhaps the creative Word or Logos, which executes the details of creation.

66
THE FORBIDDING
At-taḥrim

Most of this sura was probably revealed late in the Medinan period, and is connected with an incident, namely, that Muḥammad was found by one of his wives, Ḥafṣa, in dalliance with his slave-concubine, Mary the Copt, on a day that 'belonged' to Ḥafṣa (or 'Ā'isha), according to his custom of assigning to each a day in turn. The date of this event is uncertain. It has been argued that, since there is no mention of Mary's son Ibrāhīm, the incident must have been prior to his birth (and her pregnancy?); and the birth of Ibrāhīm was possibly about April 630. Muḥammad's difficulties with his wives, however, may have been due to his increased wealth after the conquest of Mecca and victory of Ḥunayn in January 630, and so a date after the birth of Ibrāhīm might seem more likely.

1 – 5 Muḥammad and his wives

1 *seeking the good pleasure of thy wives:* that is, seeking their approval; this probably refers to the incident with Mary, though there is also a story of how, after one of his wives had given him a dish of honey which he greatly liked, three others said he smelt.

2 *the absolution of your oaths:* while the words are ostensibly addressed to all Muslims, there may be a special reference to an oath Muḥammad is said to have made to Ḥafṣa after the incident described, namely, that he would never touch Mary again; the word translated 'absolution' (*taḥilla*) probably means not merely annulment or loosing but also an expiation for annulment; cf. 5.89/91.

3 a certain matter: to pacify Ḥafṣa after her discovery of the incident, Muḥammad is said to have told some secret to her—in some versions that he would be succeeded by Abū-Bakr ('Ā'isha's father) and 'Umar (her father)—and she then told this to 'Ā'isha.

4 if you two repent to God: sc. Ḥafṣa and 'Ā'isha; the sense is 'if you repent, good and well'.

against him: sc. Muḥammad.

5 if he divorces you: addressed to all Muḥammad's wives; Muḥammad at one time withdrew from all his wives for a month, and threatened to divorce them; this may have been partly due to the incident with Mary, partly to other things; at the end of the month he said he was willing to take them back, but presented them with 'the verse of the choice' (33.28). A full and scholarly account of these matters will be found in Nabia Abbott, *Aishah the Beloved of Mohammed* (Chicago, 1942), 44–59.

6 – 12 Believers and unbelievers

6 stones: cf. comment on 2.24/2.

8 their light: cf. 57.12.

10 for the unbelievers: the grammatical form is masculine so that both men and women are included; it has been suggested that verses 10–12 are earlier than 1–5; they may have been added to this sura since it deals with the prophet's wives, but the similitude is for all believers.

the wife of Noah: cf. comment on 11.40/2.

11 the wife of Pharaoh: Muslim tradition has stories of how she was tortured.

12 she confirmed the Words: or 'believed'; cf. *Luke*, 1.38,45 where the latter verse has 'blessed is she that believed'.

67

THE KINGDOM

Al-mulk

Probably mainly of the later Meccan period.

1 – 5 God as creator of the heavens

5 *Things to store:* said to be shooting stars, cf. 15, 18.

6 – 12 Rewards of unbelievers and believers

13 – 30 God's wisdom and power

68

THE PEN

Al-qalam

Mainly Meccan from the middle period when Muḥammad's opponents were making verbal attacks and trying to get him to agree to a compromise.

1 – 9 Muḥammad's mission genuine

1 the Pen, and what they inscribe: sometimes taken as a reference to the Pen mentioned in Tradition, which fixed a man's life beforehand. It is more likely, however, that the reference is to previous scriptures; and 'they' may be angels or prophets. The existence of scriptures is a confirmation of Muḥammad's mission.

4 a mighty morality: also taken to be 'of a noble disposition' or '(engaged) in a mighty task' (*sc.* reciting the Qur'ān).

9 compromise: e.g. by agreeing not to attack idolatry, if he himself is not attacked.

10 – 16 An opponent to be despised

13 ignoble: usually said to mean 'adopted from an ignoble family', but perhaps designating some old relationship.

17 – 33 Parable of the devastated garden

(This reflects the presumptuous attitude of many leading Meccans.)

18 the saving words: that is, the phrase 'if God will', which is much used by Muslims in referring to future events; cf. 18.24/3.

34 – 43 The fate of the unbelievers

35 Those who have surrendered: or 'The Muslims'.

39 oaths: that is, guaranteeing their safety.

41 associates: that is, deities associated with God.

42 when the leg shall be bared: that is, a day of war or other calamity—a metaphor found in poetry.

43 bow themselves: prostrate themselves in worship.

44 – 47 God's treatment of unbelievers

48 – 52 Muḥammad to be patient and firm

48 The Man of the Fish: Jonah.

69
THE INDUBITABLE
Al-ḥāqqa

This sura belongs to the early Meccan period.

1 – 12 Destruction of unbelieving peoples

1 *The Indubitable:* literally, what is due or owed, or what is bound to come; the reference is to punishment for misdeeds.

4 *Clatterer:* cf. sura 101, where it is 'the hour'.

5 *Screamer:* said to be fire from heaven, but intentionally vague.

9 *those before him:* perhaps Noah and his family.

13 – 18 The terror of the Last Day

19 – 37 The judgement on good and wicked

19 *book:* the record of his deeds.

37 *foul pus:* so some commentators, but the precise meaning seems to have been unknown.

38 – 52 The truth of Muḥammad's message affirmed

38/39 by what you see: the point may be that visible and invisible equally exist, and the message comes from the invisible.

40 Messenger: Muḥammad.

51 the truth of certainty: that is, the Qur'ān is certainly true.

70

THE STAIRWAYS

Al-ma'ārij

The sura is Meccan with the possible exception of one or two verses (such as 30) which may be Medinan. The exact dating, however, is uncertain.

1 – 18 The imminent Punishment

1 a questioner: usually taken to be a critic or sceptic (Dawood), and identified with an-Nadr ibn-al-Ḥārith or Abū-Jahl (al-Bayḍāwī), who said in effect 'If this is true, let it happen'.

3 Stairways: sometimes taken as those by which prayers and good actions mount up to God, and this is supported by v. 4 (probably later); some earlier commentators took it as 'sublimity' or 'favours'.

19 – 35 Impatience and piety described

26 confirm: count true.

30 what their right hands own: slave-concubines.

32 trusts: keep what is entrusted to them, and fulfil covenants.

36 – 44 Advances of unbelievers rejected

This passage seems to refer to some definite incident, but no record appears to have been preserved apart from vague stories about Meccans hoping to enter Paradise without believing in Muḥammad and his message, or crowding round him to bait him.

71

NOAH

Nūḥ

Middle Meccan period, reflecting the experiences of Muḥammad more than those of the Biblical Noah.

1 – 7/6 Noah's mission to his people

8/7 – 20/19 Noah's sermon

11/10 loose heaven . . . in torrents: send rain abundantly; this is a promise, not a threat.

14/13 in stages: usually taken of the embryo, but might also refer to the various ages of man.

19/18 carpet: has the connotation of 'spreading widely'.

20/19 thread ways, ravines: or 'pass along spacious paths'; the general reference is to possibilities for trade.

21/0 – 28/9 Noah's rejection

It is to be noted that the rejection of the prophet is accompanied by a return to pagan worship.

23/2 f. Wadd, Suwā', Yaghūth, Ya'ūq, Nasr: deities worshipped in Arabia in Muḥammad's time, mainly by tribes of South Arabian origin.

72
THE JINN
Al-jinn

This sura is said to have been revealed shortly after Muḥammad's visit to aṭ-Ṭā'if about 621, since as he was on his way back to Mecca a company of jinn are said to have been converted by his preaching.

1 – 15 Speech of the jinn

8 guards, meteors: angels were supposed to drive away demons by throwing shooting-stars at them; cf. 15.18.

16 – 19 Belief and unbelief

16 Would they . . .: either God or angels speaking.

19 the servant of God: Muḥammad; 'they' is usually taken of the jinn.

20 – 28 Answers to be given to opponents

23/4 Deliverance: i.e. proclamation.

27 watchers: angels who record whether the Messenger has fulfilled his tasks.

73
THE ENWRAPPED ONE
Al-muzzammil

Early Meccan, apart from v. 20 which is generally agreed to be Medinan.

1 – 14 Muḥammad urged to night-watches

1 enwrapped: it has been suggested that Muḥammad did this for protection from supernatural powers, or to induce revelations; cf. 74.1.

4 chant: now understood of formal cantillation.

5 a weighty word: said to be weighty because the commands were difficult to carry out.

6 heavier in tread: an obscure phrase, perhaps meaning 'more efficacious for steadfast continuance, *sc.* in devotion' (Sale). The general sense is that Muḥammad (and his followers) should have time at night for quiet meditation, since they are fully occupied by day.

10 forsake: from the same root as Hijra, and meaning 'break off ties' or 'have no friendly dealings with them', but probably not yet implying that Muḥammad was to leave Mecca.

15 – 19 Appeal to unbelievers to believe

18 its promise: the promise of such a day; it may also be translated 'His promise'.

20 The abrogation of night-vigils

cancelling the command in vv. 2 ff., since at Medina Muḥammad had much business to transact.

20 number it: i.e. exactly, or so as not to do more than necessary.

turned: i.e. favourably.

mightier a wage: greater as a wage or reward.

74

SHROUDED

Al-muddaththir

Some early Muslim authorities considered this the first sura to be revealed, presumably because 'rise and warn' (v. 2) is appropriate for the beginning of a ministry. The commoner view was that the first revelation was the beginning of 96; some then said that 74 followed, but after a gap in the revelations. There seems to be little connection between different sections of this sura, but it is mostly early Meccan.

1 – 10 Muḥammad exhorted to prepare for the Last Day

1 *shrouded in thy mantle:* Ar. *muddaththir,* meaning 'enmantled'.

3 *magnify:* Ar. *kabbir,* which later means, 'say, God is most great'.

5 *defilement:* or punishment (as an expression of God's anger) or idolatry; cf. *Journal of Semitic Studies*, ii, 360–65, *Early Islam*, 71-4.

11 – 26 God's dealing with an opponent

11 *him whom I created:* traditionally al-Walīd ibn-al-Mughīra, one of the leading merchants of Mecca.

16 *forward unto:* that is, stubbornly rejects.

17 hard ascent: said to be a metaphor for calamities.

18 determined: usually interpreted as 'plotted' or 'planned'.

26 Sakar: Ar. Saqar, a proper name for Hell, with the suggestion of 'scorching'.

27 – 31/4 Hell and its guards

30 nineteen: that is, angel guards; the rest of this section, sometimes regarded as one verse, sometimes divided into four, must be a later addition after the mysterious number nineteen had caused arguments.

31/3 those in whose hearts there is sickness: the name given before the battle of Uḥud to those who afterwards were called 'hypocrites'—an indication that this passage is Medinan.

31/4 it: the Qur'ān.

32/5 – 48/9 The Qur'ān: the fate of the unbelievers

38/41 what it has earned: its acts as leading to reward or punishment.

39/41 Companions of the Right: presumably the blessed, but it is sometimes said to be those who were not judged by their acts, such as angels or infants.

45/6 plunged: usually said to imply 'into discussion'.

49/50 – 56/5 Attitude to the Reminder

75
THE RESURRECTION
Al-qiyāma

Various separate Meccan passages, mostly early.

1 – 6 God's power to raise the dead

2 reproachful: Ar. *lawwāma,* that is, blaming itself on the Last Day for neglecting the message; or (of a pious soul) 'blaming others'; the precise meaning is uncertain, but the phrase was used by later mystical writers.

7 – 15 The Last Day

13 former . . . latter: that is, all his deeds.

16 – 19 The reciting of the Qur'ān

17 to recite it: literally, 'the reciting (*qur'ān*) of it'.

18 follow: seems to imply Muḥammad heard it recited.

19 explain: literally, 'to make clear'.

20 – 30 The neglectful have to meet death and judgement

20 hasty: hastening away, and so the fleeting or temporal world.

23 *gazing:* often taken to prove that in Paradise one of the chief joys is the vision of God.

26 *it:* the soul as it departs at death.

27 *enchanter:* or worker of charms to save the man's life.

29 *leg . . . with leg:* perhaps describes the dying man's inability to move his legs.

31 – 35 A supercilious opponent

31 *confirmed . . . not:* did not believe the warning.

34 *nearer:* also interpreted 'woe to thee', but in either case the reference is obscure.

36 – 40 Creation shows God's power to raise the dead

36 *to roam at will:* often interpreted 'without obligations'.

76

MAN

Al-insān

Probably Meccan, though sometimes said to be Medinan.

1 – 3 The creation of man

2 mingling: probably refers to the union of male and female elements.

trying him: perhaps in the sense of giving him experience through various stages of life.

4 – 22 The reward of the pious

5 camphor: sometimes said to be the name of a fountain in Paradise, Kāfūr.

16 have measured very exactly: an obscure phrase perhaps meaning that those in Paradise have a size of goblet determined by their wish or by the good deeds they have done.

23 – 26 Muḥammad to be patient and worship

23 a sending down: often interpreted as 'gradually' or in separate portions.

26 *bow down:* in prostration.

27 – 31 Attitudes to the Last Day and the Reminder

27 *leave behind:* disregard the Day of Judgement.

28 *exchange:* substitute their likes for them.

29 *this:* the Qur'ān.

77
THE LOOSED ONES
Al-mursalāt

This sura has more unity than many since it is concerned with the certainty and the terror of the Last Day, while verses 14 to 50 have a kind of refrain. It belongs to the early or middle Meccan period.

1 – 7 The certainty of the Judgement

1 loosed ones: or 'those that are sent'; the first five verses have feminine plural participles, whose reference has been much discussed. It has been suggested that the first three verses describe rain clouds and the fourth and fifth destructive winds; but another possible view is that all refer to angels.

8 – 15 The signs of the Last Day

11 time: that is, probably, for interceding for their followers.

13 Day of Decision: or 'of separation', that is, of the unbelievers from the believers; Ar. *faṣl.*

16 – 50 Description of the Day of Decision

19, 20 water ... lodging: seed, the womb.

30 *shadow:* said to be from the smoke of Hell in three columns.

32 *dry faggots:* or 'like a castle'.

33 *golden herds:* that is, of camels.

78
THE TIDING
An-naba'

Probably from the early or middle Meccan period.

1 – 5 The certainty of Judgement

1 they: unbelievers, or unbelievers and believers jointly.

6 – 16 Signs of God's power

6 cradle: something spread out flat.

12 seven strong ones: or 'firm ones'; the seven heavens.

13 lamp: the sun.

17 – 41 The Last Day

25 boiling water and pus: meaning not certain; cf. 38.57.

29 a book: the record of a man's deeds.

37 of whom they have no power to speak: or 'whom they have no right of addressing'.

38 save him to whom . . . given leave: that is (probably) to speak as an intercessor.

41 have forwarded: sc. his good and bad deeds.

79

THE PLUCKERS

An-nāzi'āt

Early to middle Meccan.

1 – 14 The Resurrection

1 those that pluck out: here as in 77 the feminine plural participles are capable of several meanings and interpretations; the reference is perhaps to angels or to steeds.

12 a losing return: that is, being restored to life is a disadvantage.

15 – 26 Moses and Pharaoh

19 then thou shalt fear: or 'that thou mightest fear'.

20 the great sign: presumably the turning of his staff into a serpent as in 7.107/104.

23 mustered: sc. his people.

25 the Last World and the First: literally, 'the last and the first', but probably meaning the world to come and this world.

27 – 33 God's power in creation

27 are you stronger . . .: or 'are you more difficult to create?'

29 forenoon: the morning when it has reached its full brightness; cf. 93.1.

34 – 41 The judgement

36 advanced: set out in front for spectators to see.

40 Station: that is, the standing before God to be judged.
caprice: vain desire.

42 – 46 The date of Judgement

42 berth: or simply 'come'.

80

HE FROWNED

'Abasa

Separate early Meccan passages.

1 – 10 Muḥammad and the blind man

2 that: or 'because'; the story is that while Muḥammad was talking to some leading members of Quraysh and had hopes of their conversion, a blind man, 'Abd-Allāh ibn-Umm-Maktūm, interrupted him and asked for teaching, and at this Muḥammad frowned and turned away. Details of the story have been questioned, but it is unlikely that any later Muslims would have completely invented such a story. Ibn-Umm-Maktūm was not poor but belonged to the moderately important clan of 'Āmir.

3 what should teach thee?: how can you know whether he will purify himself or not?

cleanse: or 'purify'; implies belief in the message conveyed by Muḥammad.

7 concern: or 'responsibility'.

11 – 16/15 The sublimity of the message

17/16 – 32 Man's ingratitude and God's goodness

20 the way eased: sc. from the womb; or the way through life by the sending of guidance.

26 split the earth: describes plants thrusting shoots through caked earth.

28 reeds: rather 'clover'.

33 – 42 The Last Day

81
THE DARKENING
At-takwīr

Two early Meccan passages.

1 – 14 The Last Day

4 pregnant camels: literally 'tenners' or 'ten-monthers'; it is said that it was at the tenth month that she-camels with young required most attention.

7 coupled: usually said to mean 'joined with their bodies', but perhaps better 'joined with their likes'.

8 buried infant: Ar. *maw'ūda* (fem.); this is part of the evidence that among the pre-Islamic Arabs unwanted female children were buried alive; cf. 16.58/60f.; but the extent of the practice should not be exaggerated.

10 the scrolls: the record of men's deeds.

15 – 29 The truth of the Message (in reply to attacks by Meccan pagans)

15 slinkers: this and the other terms following are usually applied to stars; the 'slinkers' are the planets because they sometimes seem to move backwards.

19 Messenger: identified with Gabriel as the bringer of revelation, though the word 'Messenger' (*rasūl*) was later applied specially to Muḥammad.

23 *he truly saw him:* a reference to the vision described more fully in 53.1–12.

24 *niggardly of:* unwilling to communicate what he has learnt; a variant reading (*ẓanīn* for *ḍanīn*) would mean 'nor does he hold baseless opinions of'.

27, 29 *all being*(*s*)*:* literally, 'the worlds'.

82
THE SPLITTING
Al-infitār

Early Meccan.

1 – 5 The Last Day

4 overthrown: that is, by the coming to life of the bodies in them.

5 the former and the latter: literally 'what it has advanced and what retarded'; other interpretations are possible.

6 – 12 Man's ingratitude and unbelief

10 watchers: recording angels.

13 – 19 Judgement and its outcome

19 soul: that is, person; not distinguished here from body; at the judgement a man cannot be helped by numerous or influential kinsmen.

83
THE STINTERS
Al-muṭaffifīn

Probably from the middle Meccan period.

1 – 6 False measure

2 measure against: that is, weigh out what they themselves are to receive, as distinct from what the people are to receive, for in the latter case they make the quantity less than it ought to be; this may refer either to exchange of one kind of goods for another, or to exchange of goods for money (which has to be weighed).

3 a mighty day: the day of judgement, where the use made of money and goods will be taken into consideration.

7 – 17 The libertines

7 Sijjīn: the meaning is uncertain; it could conceivably be an intensive form of the word *sijn*, 'prison', and mean Hell or some part of it; or it might mean a scroll.

14 that they were earning: probably means simply 'what they were doing' as being credited to their account, but not specifically wages or profits.

rusted: and so dulled their perceptions.

15 veiled: or 'curtained off from'.

18 – 28 The pious

18 illiyun: Ar. *'illiyyīn*; of uncertain meaning, though seems to be connected with the root meaning 'high', 'up'; in any case it is contrasted with Sijjīn.

27 Tasnīm: of uncertain meaning.

29 – 36 Believers and unbelievers

84
THE RENDING
Al-inshiqāq

Mostly early Meccan.

1 – 15 The Judgement

2 is fitly disposed: sc. for the appearance of God; or it might be translated 'humbly submits'.

4 what is in it: the dead bodies.

11 call for destruction: invoke destruction on himself.

14 revert: that is, from prosperity to misery.

16 – 19 Changes

This short and mysterious passage is usually taken of the various stages of a man's life; but it might perhaps refer to the succession of generations in a whole society.

20 – 25 The critics of the Qur'ān

24 give them good tidings: or simply 'give them tidings'.

85
THE CONSTELLATIONS
Al-burūj

Probably early Meccan passages; but verses 8 to 11 seem to be later.

1 – 9 The Men of the Pit

2 *the promised day:* perhaps the Day of Judgement, and in that case the Fire (v. 5) may be Hell.

3 *the witness ...:* there is no satisfactory interpretation.

4 *slain were ...:* also taken as a wish or curse, 'slain be ...'.

the Men of the Pit: literally, 'the owners or lords of the pit'. These are often said to be the followers of a Jewish king in the Yemen, Dhū-Nuwās, who in 523 persecuted those Christians of Najrān who refused to abjure their faith, and is said to have burnt them in a pit or trench. Some Muslim commentators made the reference to the fiery furnace of *Daniel,* ch. 3; and there were also other stories. Some modern scholars make the passage refer to Hell, and then 'witnesses' in v. 7 means that those punished bear witness against themselves.

10, 11 The recompense of persecutors and righteous

12 – 22 Various short passages

22 guarded tablet: or 'preserved in a tablet'. The tablet is commonly understood to be in heaven and to contain the original of the Qur'ān (Ar. *lawḥ maḥfūẓ*).

86

THE NIGHT-STAR

Aṭ-ṭāriq

Seems to consist of short passages, mostly early.

1 night-star: literally, coming at night or suddenly; the occasion of the revelation of the passage is sometimes said to have been the anxiety of Muḥammad's uncle Abū-Ṭālib after seeing a shooting-star.

3 piercing: fits the reference to a shooting-star.

4 watcher: presumably a guardian angel, especially since shooting-stars were thought to be thrown by demons against the angels guarding heaven, cf. 37.6–10; but some Muslims thought the watcher was God.

6 gushing water: human seed.

8 He is able: God has power to restore man to life for judgement since he had power to create him originally.

10 no helper: an Arab normally relied on his kinsmen to help him when his case was judged.

11 rain: the rain comes when the stars have returned to a certain position.

12 splitting: the shoots are regarded as splitting the hard earth.

13 it: the message.

16 I am devising: man proposes and God disposes.

87
THE MOST HIGH
Al-aʻla

The first half is early Meccan; the rest is probably a little later.

1 – 8 God supports Muḥammad in recitation

3 determined: sc. the species with their distinctive qualities; or predetermined the destiny of each.

guided: especially by revelation.

5 blackening wrack: describes the dead and decaying vegetation in the wadis.

6 recite: sc. the Qur'ān.

8 the Easing: ease in remembering the Qur'ān, or the easy religion, viz. Islam.

9 – 19 Attitudes to the Reminder

10 fears: sc. God.

remember: that is, accept the Reminder.

14 cleansed himself: Ar. *tazakkā,* meaning that he followed Muḥammad's religious practices, which may also have included almsgiving; cf. *Mecca,* 165–9.

19 scrolls of Abraham: Muslims regard Abraham as a prophet or messenger, and so the recipient of a revelation which has been written down, although there is no mention of this in the Bible.

88

THE ENVELOPER

Al-ghāshiya

Early Meccan.

1 – 16 Hell and Paradise

1 Enveloper: the enveloping or overwhelming day when mankind is judged; *ghāshiya* is a feminine participle.

9 striving: actions in this world and their result.

17 – 20 God's power

17 camel: Ar. *ibl,* which can also mean 'clouds'.

21 – 26 Warning to the unbelievers

21 reminder: one who reminds or warns.

22 oversee: that is, Muḥammad only conveys a message and has no authority.

89
THE DAWN
Al-fajr

Early to middle Meccan.

1 – 5/4 An oath

No satisfactory explanation of the references has been given. The verse 'Is there . . . man?' may be regarded as parenthetic, and the following passage as the assertion supported by the oath.

6/5 – 14/13 The punishment of disobedient peoples

7/6 Iram: in apposition with 'Ad' and perhaps best taken as their city or territory, where there was a magnificent palace or temple; hence the 'pillars'. 'Ad' here is said to be 'the former Ad'.

9/8 valley: identified with Wādi-l-qurā near Medina where dwellings were cut out of the rock.

10/9 tent-pegs: not satisfactorily explained.

15/14 – 20/1 Man's attitude to wealth and poverty

19/20 inheritance: sc. of which you are trustee; this whole passage describes the sins of the rich Meccans.

21/2 – 30 Description of the Judgement

24/5 forwarded: that is, had performed good acts in this world which would have ensured life in Paradise.

90
THE LAND
Al-balad

Early Meccan.

1 – 7 Man's humble birth and his pride

2 *lodger:* or resident; the precise reference is obscure.

4 *in trouble:* 'subject to trouble', or 'by a painful process'.

8 – 17 Upright conduct

10 *the two highways:* may be the paths of good and evil, of which the former would be 'the steep'. The points mentioned are similar to those in 89.17/18 ff.

18 – 20 Those on the right and left

91
THE SUN
Ash-shams

Early Meccan.

1 – 10 Prosperity and failure

1 By the sun: the point of the oath is the contrast of sun and moon, day and night, heaven (sky) and earth.

2 she follows him: the difference of gender helps the understanding of the passage, but in Arabic the sun is feminine and the moon masculine.

8 lewdness and godfearing: its wicked and pious acts; the verse has troubled Muslim commentators, who hold that God commands only good, although he 'creates' both the good and bad acts of men.

9 purifies: zakkā-hā, cf. 87.14.

11 – 15 The punishment of Thamood

12 the most wretched: or 'miserable'; usually taken to be the most wicked who was leader in disobedience; but the word translated 'uprose' can also be 'was sent (as a messenger)', and would then refer to the Messenger in the next verse. This might imply, however, that Muḥammad was 'wretched' in Mecca.

14 levelled: usually interpreted as 'overwhelmed or punished all alike'.

15 the issue: presumably the consequence by way of retaliation.

92
THE NIGHT
Al-layl

Early Meccan.

1 – 13 The diverse paths

1 By the night . . .: the oath, as in sura 91, points contrasts.

3 That which created: the creator can only be God, but the apparent use of an impersonal pronoun has caused great discussions among commentators, and there are several variant readings; in any case the emphasis is not on the creative activity but on the resulting contrast.

6 confirms: takes as true the teaching about Paradise.

8 self-sufficient: considers himself independent of higher powers because of his wealth.

14 – 21 Warning of the flaming Fire

14 Fire: that is, Hell.

18 to purify: cf. 87.14.

20 seeking the Face of: roughly equivalent to 'for the sake of . . .'.

93
THE FORENOON
Aḍ-ḍuḥā

Early Meccan.

1 – 11 God's favour to Muḥammad

1 white forenoon: Ar. *ḍuḥā,* which means the part of the day between dawn and midday when the sun has become hot.

3 has neither forsaken thee . . .: the sura is said to have been revealed when Muḥammad was despondent because no revelation came, but the circumstances are differently described; the message is clearly one of encouragement.

6 orphan: Muḥammad was a posthumous child, and his mother died when he was six.

7 erring: this is how Muḥammad must have regarded his earlier religious position; it does necessarily imply active participation in idolatrous worship, for many Meccans had a vaguely monotheistic outlook, and may simply mean absence of positive knowledge of God's nature and commands.

8 needy: minors inherited nothing, and in any case most of Muḥammad's relatives were poor, so that he virtually had nothing until his marriage with Khadīja; God is regarded as 'sufficing' or enriching him through this marriage.

9 do not oppress . . .: gratitude for God's goodness is to be expressed in practical ways.

94
THE EXPANDING
Ash-sharaḥ

Probably early Meccan. Like the preceding sura, with which it may be connected, it gives Muḥammad encouragement and reassurance.

1 expand: in order to make possible the receiving of spiritual truth; this is the usual interpretation, but some commentators took it as a reference to the 'opening' of Muḥammad's breast when a child by angels in order to remove the black clot of sin.

2 burden: often taken as the burden of sins committed before he became Messenger of God; but it could also be ignorance or distress of mind or, if the sura is later, the strain of leading his community.

7 empty: or free, perhaps on the completion of preaching or prayer.

labour: that is (possibly), to serve God.

95

THE FIG

Aṭ-ṭīn

Early Meccan.

1 *By the fig and the olive:* presumably named because they help man to maintain life and make it pleasanter.

3 *this land secure:* the *ḥaram* or sanctuary of Mecca.

5 *lowest of the low:* the reference is probably to the decrepitude of old age or to death. The point would then be that, as God has power to give man a pleasant life, and then take it away, so He has power to restore him to life for judgement. Others refer 'lowest of the low' to man's moral baseness or punishment in Hell.

7 *cry thee lies:* disbelieve thy (Muḥammad's) proclamation of judgement.

96
THE BLOOD-CLOT
Al-'alaq

Early Meccan. According to the most widely received Traditions, verses 1 to 8 are the first revelation; but this may be an inference of later scholars from the logical priority of the command to 'recite', *iqra'*, since this word is from the same root as Qur'ān.

1 – 8 Muḥammad to proclaim his revelations

2 *blood-clot:* the early form of the embryo in the womb.

3 *recite: And thy Lord . . .:* or 'recite, since thy Lord . . .'.

5 *that he knew not:* what he did not know—presumably through earlier scriptures.

6 *insolent:* or presumptuous, thinking he is not subordinate to any higher power.

self-sufficient: cf. 92.8.

8 *Returning: sc.* to God for judgement.

9 – 19 Muslim worship opposed

9 *he who forbids:* said to be Abū-Jahl, Muḥammad's most vigorous opponent at Mecca in the years before the Hijra and until his death at Badr in 624.

10 a servant: or slave, *sc.* of God, and probably referring to Muḥammad, on whose neck Abū-Jahl had threatened to put his foot if he found him prostrating himself in worship.

11 upon guidance: following what has been revealed.

17 concourse: those who associate with him and might be expected to support him.

18 guards of Hell: so usually interpreted, but obscure.

97
POWER
Al-qadr

Early Meccan.

1 sent it down: the Qur'ān, on the usual view. Since the Qur'ān was sent down or revealed over a period of more than twenty years, it is held that on this night the whole Qur'ān was taken from the 'guarded tablet' (85.22) beside God's throne to the lowest of the seven heavens, and from this position taken by the angels to Muḥammad as occasion required.

Night of Power: or perhaps 'of the Decree'. Muḥammad is believed to have received the first revelation on this night. It is held to be one of the last ten nights of the month of Ramaḍān.

4 the spirit: usually identified with Gabriel.

upon every command: or 'concerning every matter'.

98
THE CLEAR SIGN
Al-bayyina

Medinan, presumably after Badr.

1 – 5/4 The Clear Sign

1 would never leave off: obscure; it is sometimes said to mean that they had promised to follow the truth when a Messenger came, but on Muḥammad's appearance they rejected him.

2 a Messenger: sc. Muḥammad; the word is in apposition with 'Clear Sign'.

3/2 true: or 'eternal' (*qayyima*).

4/3 scattered not: or 'became divided'; said to mean that some acknowledged Muḥammad to be the prophet foretold, while others did not.

5/4 sincerely: in single-mindedness.

religion of the True: Ar. *dīn al-qayyima*, perhaps 'of the eternal truth', and so 'the right religion'.

6/5 – 8 Unbelievers and believers

99
THE EARTHQUAKE
Az-zalzala

Early Meccan, though sometimes thought Medinan.

1 *shaking:* the earthquake as a prelude of the Last Day.

2 *burdens:* what is buried in it, bodies especially.

6 *in scatterings:* in separate groups.
to see: literally 'to be shown'.

100

THE CHARGES

Al-'ādiyāt

Meccan.

1 *the snorting chargers:* the opening passages contain only feminine participles, adjectives or verbs, and they are usually referred to war-horses, though this interpretation is not certain.

2 *strikers of fire:* with their hooves on stones.

4 *blazing:* raising and leaving behind them.

5 *cleaving there:* said to mean that they pass through the enemy in the dust-cloud.

7 *against that:* he is a witness to his ingratitude.

8 *passionate:* said to imply niggardliness.

9 *is overthrown:* brought out in disorderly fashion; this happens on the Last Day.

10 *brought out:* men's inmost thoughts are made manifest.

11 *aware:* fully informed.

101

THE CLATTERER

Al-qāri'a

Meccan.

1 The Clatterer: in Arabic a feminine participle meaning 'clattering', 'striking' or 'knocking at the door'. The reference is to a happening on the Last Day; cf. 69.4.

2 The day: adverbial, that is 'The Clatterer will make a clatter on the day . . .'.

6/5, 8/6 weigh heavy, weigh light: presumably means that the good deeds weigh more or less than the evil deeds.

9/6 in the womb of the Pit: variously interpreted, but the literal meaning probably is 'his mother is the Pit'.

102

RIVALRY

At-takāthur

Meccan (probably).

1 rivalry: especially an emulous desire to multiply one's wealth.

2 the tombs: the thought is that man can take nothing with him into the grave.

8 true bliss: literally 'the pleasant'; it could also mean the pleasures they had experienced in this life.

103

AFTERNOON

Al-'aṣr

Early Meccan, but verse 3 may be a much later addition.

1 afternoon: Ar. *'aṣr*, the hour of one of the five prayers; but the word also means 'time' generally, and this would fit better the idea of loss.

104
THE BACKBITER
Al-humaza

Meccan, said to have been revealed after verbal attacks on Muḥammad by al-Akhnas ibn-Sharīq or Umayya ibn-Khalaf or al-Walīd ibn-al-Mughīra.

1 backbiter, slanderer: the form indicates that he habitually acted in this way.

2 counted them over: implying that he regarded them as provision against future calamities.

4 Crusher: sometimes taken as a proper name, al-Ḥuṭama, whose mysterious character might cause terror.

8 covered down: the picture is apparently of an arched vault supported on columns.

105
THE ELEPHANT
Al-fīl

Meccan. It is said to refer to an expedition of the Abyssinian ruler of the Yemen, Abraha, against Mecca about the year 570.

1 *Men of the Elephant:* Abraha's army, so called because they had one or more elephants.

2 *go astray:* the expedition may have been planned to destroy the Ka'ba and so reduce Mecca's trade (to the advantage of a new Christian church at Ṣan'ā'), but it completely failed in this aim.

4 *stones of baked clay:* each bird is alleged to have carried three stones, one in its beak and one in each foot, and to have dropped these on the Abyssinian army. Each stone is said to have hit the man whose name was written on it.

106

KORAISH

Quraysh

Early Meccan. It is sometimes joined to the sura of the Elephant (105) to make one sura.

1 the composing: may be understood in several ways, e.g. of the union and harmony among the people of Mecca, or their ability to assemble caravans for long-distance trade. The first two verses may also be taken with the following verses as giving the reason for praising God; or (when connected with the previous verse) they may state the purpose to be attained by God's frustrating the Abyssinians.

Koraish: Ar. Quraysh, the tribe inhabiting Mecca.

2 the winter and summer caravan: Mecca had become a great trading centre. It is said the winter caravan went south to the Yemen and Abyssinia, and the summer caravan to Syria.

3 serve: or 'worship'.

the Lord of this House: the deity worshipped in the Ka'ba, here identified with God. This apparent acceptance by the Qur'ān of pre-Islamic worship is probably to be explained by a growing belief among the more intelligent Meccans that worship at the Ka'ba was directed towards the supreme deity, even if they still acknowledge minor objects of worship, semi-divine or angelic.

4/3 has fed them: Mecca was prosperous through trade, though the region was barren.

4 secured them: through establishing the sacred character of Mecca and the surrounding territory.

107

CHARITY

Al-mā'ūn

Date uncertain. Traditionally verses 1 to 3 are Meccan, the rest Medinan.

1 *repulses the orphan:* the connection of such conduct, and of failing to feed the needy, with denial of the Judgement suggests the early Meccan period.

7 *refuse charity:* do not give *zakāt* or alms. Such is the traditional interpretation, but the Arabic word *mā'ūn* is of uncertain meaning. Other meanings suggested are 'necessaries' or 'help, succour'; but it may be connected with a Hebrew word meaning 'refuge'. If the meaning is general, the second part of the sura might also be Meccan.

108
ABUNDANCE
Al-kawthar

Date uncertain, but traditionally Meccan. It gives Muḥammad encouragement when insulted.

1 *abundance:* could mean wealth or followers.

2 *sacrifice:* if the sura is early, this might mean taking part in pre-Islamic rites at the Ka'ba, but, since the Qur'ān regards the Ka'ba as a sanctuary of God, this is not reprehensible. This is the only use of the root *naḥara* in the Qur'ān, but the sacrifice of an animal is part of the rites of the greater pilgrimage (*ḥajj*).

3 *the one cut off:* Ar. *al-abtar*, used of an animal with its tail docked. It is said Muḥammad had been mocked because he had no surviving sons.

109

THE UNBELIEVERS

Al-kāfirūn

Meccan.

1 Say: what follows is the reply to be given by Muḥammad to certain Meccans who tried to persuade him to pay some respect to their gods, as he was apparently prepared to do at the time of the 'satanic verses'; cf. 53.19,20.

6 to you your religion: there is to be no compromise.

110

HELP

An-naṣr

Medinan. Traditionally the last sura to be revealed; this was during the Pilgrimage of Farewell, about three months before Muḥammad's death. Some modern scholars think it earlier.

1 victory: Ar. *fat'ḥ*, literally 'opening', often applied to the conquest of Mecca, but in 8.19 to the victory at Badr.

3 turns again: is ready to forgive or relent.

III

PERISH

Tabbat

Traditionally Meccan, but perhaps Medinan. The reason for the bitter attack on Muḥammad's uncle, Abū-Lahab, is that he became chief of the clan of Hāshim about 619 and found a justification for refusing to continue clan-protection to Muḥammad. This precipitated the Hijra.

1 Perish!: expressing a wish or curse; but both verbs may also be taken as expressing statements. The interpretation affects the dating. A curse would naturally come at Mecca, whereas, if the reference is to Abū-Lahab's death, that was a few days after the battle of Badr in 624.

3 his wife: no satisfactory explanation is given of this verse and the next.

112

SINCERE RELIGION

Al-ikhlāṣ

Meccan, according to most Muslim commentators. It is unlikely that the original reference was to Jews and Christians.

2 *the Everlasting Refuge:* the usual interpretation of *ṣamad* but it is also rendered 'eternal', 'the only one'.

3 *has not begotten:* presumably directed against the Arabian pagan belief in 'daughters of God'.

4 *equal to Him is not any one:* he has no peers.

113
DAYBREAK
Al-falaq

Meccan. This and the following sura are together known as the Mu'awwidhatān, 'the (suras) of taking refuge', and are incantations or protective formulae to ward off evil. The practice of 'taking refuge with God' is commended at various points in the Qur'ān, such as 7.200/199 f., 19.18, 23.97/9 f.

3 *darkness:* sometimes said to mean an eclipse of the moon.

4 *who blow on knots:* the use of knots in magic is common, and the women are clearly casting a spell, but nothing is known of its exact character.

❧ 114 ❧

MEN

An-nās

Like 113 a formula of protection against evil, especially demonic suggestions.

1 men: human beings as distinct from jinn, etc.

4 whisperer: usually understood as Satan.

INDEX OF PROPER NAMES AND ARABIC WORDS IN THE QUR'AN

'ādiyāt ('the chargers'): 100, title
'afternoon' (Ar. *'aṣr*): 103, title
Aḥmad (equivalent of Muḥammad): 61.6
aḥqāf ('sand-dunes'): 46, title, 21/0
aḥzāb ('confederates'): 33, title
a'lā ('the most high'): 87, title
'alaq ('the blood-clot'): 96, title
'All-Merciful' (Ar. Raḥmān): 55, title
'Āl Imrān ('the house of Imran'): 3, title
an'ām ('cattle'): 6, title
anbiyā' ('prophets'): 21, title
anfāl ('spoils'): 8, title
'angels' (Ar. *malā'ika*): 35, title
'ankabūt ('spider'): 29, title
'Anṣār: *see* Helpers
'ant' (Ar. *naml*): 27, title
'apartments' (Ar. *ḥujurāt*): 49, title
Apostles (of Jesus—Ar. *ḥawāriyyūn*): 3.52/45 f.; 5.111 – 3; 61.14
Arabic (language): 12.2; 13.37; 16.103/5; 20.113/2; 26.195; 39.28/9; 41.3/2, 44; 42.7/5; 43.3/2; 46.12/11
a'rāf ('battlements'): 7, title, 46/4 – 49/7
'Arafāt: hill near Mecca, 2.198/4
'aṣr ('afternoon'): 103, title
Ayka ('thicket, grove'): *see* Thicket
Ayyūb: *see* Job
Āzar: 6.74 (Abraham's father, elsewhere not named)

Baal (idol; Ar. Ba'l): 37.125
Babylon (Ar. Bābil): 2.102/96
'backbiter' (Ar. *humaza*): 104, title
Badr (site of battle): 3.123/19
balad ('land'): 90, title
baqara ('cow'): 2, title
'battlements' (Ar. *a'rāf*): 7, title
bayyina ('clear sign'): 98, title
'Be' (word of creation; Ar. *kun*): 2.117/1; 3.47/2 (to Mary), 59/2 (of Jesus); 6.73/2; 16.40/2; 19.35/6 (of Jesus); 36.82; 40.68/70
'bee' (Ar. *naḥl*): 16, title
Bedouin(s) (Ar. *a'rāb*): 9.90/1, 97/8 – 99/100; 33.20; 48.11 – 16; 49.14
Bekka (Ar. Bakka): 3.96/0, same as Mecca, *q.v.*
'believer' (Ar. *mu'min*): 40, title
'believers' (Ar. *mu'minīn*): 23, title
'blood-clot' (Ar. *'alaq*): 96, title
burūj ('constellations'): 85, title

Cain: *see* Adam, two sons of
'cattle' (Ar. *an'ām*): 6, title

El-Lat (idol): *see* Lāt
El-'Uzza (idol): *see* 'Uzzā
Emigrants (Meccan Muslims at Medina—Ar. *muhājirīn*): (4.100/1); 9.100/1, 117/8; 24.22; 33.6; 59.8; (60.10)
'enveloper' (Ar. *ghāshiya*): 88, title
Er-Rakeem: *see* Raqīm (ar-)
Er-Rass: *see* Rass (ar-)
'enwrapped' (Ar. *muzzammil*): 73, title
Evangel (Ar. Injīl): *see* Gospel
Eve (not named, but referred to as Adam's wife): 2.35/3 f.; 7.19/18 – 23/2; 20.117/5 – 121/19; 39.6/8 (Adam not named)
'expanding' (Ar. *inshirāḥ*): 94, title
Ezra (Ar. 'Uzayr): 9.30
Ez-Zakkoum: *see* Zaqqūm (az-)

fajr ('dawn'): 89, title
falaq ('daybreak'): 113, title
fat'ḥ ('victory'): 48, title
fātiḥa ('opening'): 1, title
'fig' (Ar. *tīn*): 95, title
fīl ('elephant'): 105, title
Fir'awn: *see* Pharaoh
Fire (Ar. *nār*; i.e. Hell): frequent
'forbidding' (Ar. *taḥrīm*): 66, title
'forenoon' (Ar. *ḍuḥā*): 93, title
Furqān ('salvation'): 25, title; also 2.53/0, 185/1; 3.3/2; 8.29,41/2; 21.48/9; 25.1
fuṣṣilat ('distinguished'): 41, title

Gabriel (Ar. Jibrīl): 2.97/1 f.; 66.4
Garden(s) (Ar. *janna, jannāt*): frequent
Gehenna (Ar. Jahannam): frequent
ghāshiya ('enveloper'): 88, title
Gog (Ar. Yājūj): 18.94/3; 21.96
Goliath (Ar. Jālūt): 2.249/50 – 251/2
Gospel (Ar. Injīl): the book sent down to Jesus, 3.3/2, 48/3, 65/58; 5.46/50 f., 66/70, 68/72, 110/09; 9.111/2; 48.29; 57.27—a prophet mentioned in it, 7.157/6
'Greeks' (Ar. Rūm): 30, title, 2/1 f.
Grove, men of the: *see* Thicket
Guidance (Ar. *huḍā*): frequent

ḥadīd ('iron'): 57, title
ḥajj ('pilgrimage'): 22, title
Hāmān (associated with Pharaoh): 28.6/5, 8/7, 38; 40.24/5, 36/8
ḥaqqa ('indubitable'): 69, title

Mālik; said to be name of angel, 43.77
'man' (Ar. *insān*): 76, title
Manāt: idol, 53.20
Mārūt (angel in Babylon): 2.102/96
Marwa (hill near Mecca): 2.158/3
Mary (Ar. Maryam):
birth and upbringing, 3.35/1 – 44/39—
annunciation and birth of Jesus, 3.45/0 – 47/2; 19.16 – 33/4—
her chastity and faith, 66.12—
slandered by Jews, 4.156/5—
'son of Mary' (alone), 23.50/2; 43.58/7—
'Jesus son of Mary', 2.87/1, 253/4; 3.45/0; 4.157/6, 171/69; 5.46/50, 78/82, 110/09,112,114; 19.34/5; 33.7; 57.27; 61.6,14—
'Messiah son of Mary', 5.17/19, 72/6, 75/9; 9.31
Masīḥ: *see* Messiah
masjid: *see* Mosque
mā'ūn ('charity'): 107, title
Mecca (Ar. Makka): named only in 48.24; *see also* Bekka, Kaaba, Mosque (Holy)
Medina (Ar. *al-madīna*, 'the city'): probably used as proper name, 9.101/2, 120/1; 33.60; 63.8
see also Yathrib
'men' (Ar. *an-nās*): 114, title
'Merciful' (Ar. ar-raḥmān): 55, title
Messiah (Ar. *al-masīḥ*, i.e. Jesus):
annunciation, 3.45/0—
not killed by Jews, 4.157/6—
only a messenger, etc., not divine, 4.171/69 f.; 5.17/9, 72/6, 75/9; 9.30 f.—
see also Jesus, Mary (son of)
Michael (Ar. Mīkāl): an angel, 2.98/2
Midian (Ar. Madyan):
people to whom Shu'ayb sent, 7.85/3 – 93/1; 11.84/5 – 95/8; 29.36/5 f.—
Moses among them, 20.40/2; 28.22/1–28—
also 9.70/1; 22.44/3; 28.45
'moon' (Ar. *qamar*): 54, title
Moses (Ar. Mūsā):
his childhood, 20.36 – 40/1; 28.3/2 – 21/0—
in Midian, 28.22/1–28—
call to be a prophet and deliver Israel, 14.5 – 14/17; 19.51/2 – 53/4; 20.9/8 – 23/4; 25.35/7 f.; 26.10/9 – 17/16; 27.7–14; 28.30–5; 79.15–19—
dealings with Pharaoh, 7.103/1 – 136/2; 10.75/6–89; 20.24/5 – 76/8; 23.45/7 – 48/50; 26.18/17–51; 28.36–43; 40.23/4 – 50/3; 43.46/5–56; 51.38–40; 79.20–5—
the exodus, 7.137/3 – 141/37; (10.90); 20.77/9 – 82/4; 26.52–68—
on Sinai, 7.142/38 – 147/5, 154/3 – 157/6—

Nasr: idol, 71.23
nāzi'āt ('pluckers'): 79, title
New Testament: *see* Gospel
'night' (Ar. *layl'*): 92, title
'night journey' (*isrā'*): 17, title
'night-star' (*ṭāriq*): 86, title
nisā' ('women'): 4, title
Noah (Ar. Nūḥ): as prophet and preacher, 7.59/7 – 64/2; 10.71/2 – 73/4; 11.25/7 – 34/6; 23.23 – 30/1; 26.105–20; 37.75/3 – 82/0; 71.1 – 28/9—
people destroyed by flood, 11.36/8 – 48/50; 25.37/9; 29.14/13 f.; 54.9–17—
also 3.33/0; 4.163/1; 6.84; 7.69/7; 9.70/1; 11.89/91; 14.9; 17.3,17/18; 19.58/9; 21.76 f.; 22.42/3; 33.7; 40.5,31/2; 42.13/11; 50.12; 51.46; 53.52/3; 57.26; 66.10 (wife); (69.11/12); 71, title, 1
nūr ('light'): 24, title—'light verse', 24.35

Old Testament: *see* Torah, Psalms
'opening' (Ar. *fātiḥa*): 1, title
'ornaments' (Ar. *zukhruf*): 43, title

'pen' (Ar. *qalam*): 68, title
People of the Book (Ar. *ahl al-kitāb*): 2.105/99, 109/3; 3.64/57 f., 69/2 – 72/65, 75/68, 98/3 f., 113/09, 199/8; 4.123/2, 153/2, 159/7, 171/69; 5.15/18, 19/22, 59/64, 65/70, 68/72, 77/81; 29.46/5; 33.26; 57.29; 59.2, 11; 98.1,5
'perish' (Ar. *tabbat*): 111, title
Pharaoh (Ar. Fir'awn):
rejects mission of Moses, 7.103/1 – 137/3; 10.75/6–92; 17.101/3 – 103/5; 20.24/5–36, 42/4 – 79/81; 23.45/7 – 48/50; 26.10/9–66; 28.3/2 – 6/5, 32–42; 40.23/4 – 31/3; 43.46/5 – 57/6; 51.38–40; 79.15–25—
orders Haman to build a tower, 28.38; 40.36/8 – 38/40—
'family of Pharaoh', 'people of Pharaoh', 2.49/6 f.; 3.11/9; 7.141/37; 8.52/4, 54/6; 14.6; 40.45/8 f.; 44.17/16 – 29/8, (31/0); 54.41 f.—
also 11.96/9; 27.12; 29.39/8; 38.12/11; 50.13; 66.11 (wife); 69.9; 73.15/16; 85.18; 89.9
'pilgrimage' (Ar. *ḥajj*): 22, title
'pluckers' (Ar. *nāzi'āt*): 79, title
'poets' (Ar. *shu'arā'*): 26, title
'power' (Ar. *qadr*): 97, title
'prophets' (Ar. *anbiyā'*): 21, title
'prostration' (Ar. *sajda*): 32, title
Psalms (Ar. *zabūr*): a book given to David, 4.163/1; 17.55/7—
also, 21.105; and (Ar. *zubur* perhaps 'scriptures'), 3.184/1; 16.44/6; 23.53/5; 26.196; 35.25/3; 54.43,52

qadr ('power'): 97, title
Qāf: Arabic letter, 50, title

Salsabīl: a spring in Paradise, 76.18
'salvation' (Ar. *furqān*): 25, title; *see also* Furqān
Samaritan (Ar. Sāmirī): made golden calf, 20.85/7–96
'sand-dunes' (Ar. *aḥqāf*): 46, title
Saqar: *see* Sakar
Satan (Ar. ash-Shayṭān, 'the demon'): may be taken as a proper name in the following, 2.36/4, 168/3, 208/4, 268/71, 275/6; 3.36/1, 155/49, 175/69; 4.38/42, 60/3, 76/8, 83/5, 119/8 f.; 5.90/2 f.; 6.43, 68/7, 142/3; 7.20/19, 22/1, 27/6, 175/4, 200/199 f.; 8.11, 48/50; 12.5, 42, 100/1; 14.22/6; 16.63/5, 98/100; 17.27/9, 53/5, 64/6; 18.63/2; 19.44/5 f.; 20.120/18; 22.52/1 f.; 24.21; 25.29/31; 27.24; 28.15/14; 29.38/7; 31.21/0; 35.6; 36.60; 38.41/0; 41.36; 43.62; 47.25/7; 58.10/11, 19/20; 59.16
Saul (Ar. Ṭālūt): king of Israel, 2.247/8 – 249/50
'scatterers' (Ar. *dhāriyāt*): 51, title
shams ('sun'): 91, title
Sheba (Ar. Sabā'): a land ruled by a queen, 27.22 – 44/5; a people punished, 34, title, 15/14 – 19/18
Shechina (Ar. *sakīna*): 2.248/9; 9.26, 40; 48.4, 18, 26
'shrouded' (Ar. *muddaththir*): 74, title
Shuaib (Ar. Shu'ayb): prophet sent to Midian, 7.85/3 – 93/1; 11.84/5 – 95/8; 29.36/5 f.—sent to men of Thicket, 26.176–89
shu'arā' ('poets'): 26, title
shūrā ('counsel'): 42, title
Sijjīn: 83.7 f.
Sinai (Ar. Sīnā', Sīnīn): the mount of S., 23.20; 95.2—
also simply 'the Mount' (Ar. Ṭūr), 2.63/0, 93/87; 4.154/3; 19.52/3; 20.80/2; 28.29; 52, title, 1
'sincere religion' (Ar. *ikhlāṣ*): 102, title
Sirius (Ar. ash-Shi'rā), 53.49/50
'smoke' (Ar. *dukhān*): 44, title
Solomon (Ar. Sulaymān):
the Satans (demons) in Solomon's reign, 2.102/96—
wind and Satans or jinn subjected to him, 21.78–82; 34.12/11 – 14/13; 38.36/5 – 40/39
repents and is forgiven, 38.30/29 – 40/39—
controls birds, 27.15–21—
meets Queen of Sheba, 27.22–45—
also, 4.163/1; 6.84
'spider' (Ar. *'ankabūt*): 29, title
Spirit (Ar. *rūḥ*): Holy Spirit (*ruḥ al-qudus*) aided Jesus, 2.87/1, 253/4; 5.110/09—
Holy Spirit has sent down Qur'ān, 16.102/4—
Jesus a spirit from God, 4.171/69—
God's spirit breathed into man, 15.29; 32.9/8; 38.72; 21.91 (into Mary); 66.12 (into Mary?)—
the spirit is sent down, 16.2 (with angels); 19.17 (to Mary); 26.193

INDEX TO THE COMMENTARY

(containing proper names not in the text of the Qur'ān, Arabic words and some English equivalents, and a few selected topics).